I. dawcopy. wps   →
II. master copy. wps →

ASHES AND DIAMONDS

A. J. Murray worked for many years in the United Kingdom Civil Service. This is his first historical monograph, and reflects a lifelong interest in the relations between religion and politics. He is married, with two children and two grandchildren, James and Eloise.

ASHES AND DIAMONDS

*For that day dawns in fire and the fire
will test the worth of each man's work.*
Paul

A J MURRAY

Midnight Oil Books F. P.

MIDNIGHT OIL BOOKS FREE PRESS

First published in the United Kingdom, 2007

Copyright © Alexander Murray, 2007

D P McHutchon t/a Midnight Oil Books, 120 Commercial Street, Pathhead, Kirkcaldy, Fife, UK, KY1 2NX

www.midoil.co.uk

First Edition

10 8 6 4 2 1 3 5 7 9

For Joan

ACKNOWLEDGEMENTS

My thanks to my typist, Eleanor Rowe of WriteWord, New College Library, Edinburgh, and also to the team at Midnight Oil Books Free Press.

PREFACE

Even those faintly familiar with twentieth century Christian theology will have some sense of the talismanic influence of the writings and character of Karl Barth, a fact testified to by the profusion of university-level modules springing up concentrating on his systematic theology alone. While 'Church Dogmatics' retains a universality of theme in its exploration of Christian faith, it, together with earlier Barthian works, remain very much products of their time. That the urgency and necessity of theological writing amid the politics of post-Weimar Germany did not define its content to a greater extent is perhaps remarkable; still these same politics could not be kept out of the personal and public life of Karl Barth, the academician. A. J. Murray, through 'Ashes and Diamonds' has set about to explore Barth and convey a sense of the times. As ever with the Hitlerian years, the detail of the corrosive destruction of public and social morality, Arendt's 'banality of evil', contains an unbounded ability to horrify. The milieu that we are reminded of is above all one of persistent compromise, compromise on points of doctrine, principle and morality. Barth himself, as we discover, would not come away unscathed, and yet his is at least the attempt to cling to the stubborn righteousness through faith in Jesus Christ he felt to represent a major justification for the existence of the Church. It is difficult to leave 'Ashes and Diamonds' with either an idealised or unduly hostile view of Barth, or any lack of appreciation for the 'irresistible' surge of events at that time. Both academic theologian and enthusiast-historian will find much in such historically and psychologically aware writing to commend it.

David McHutchon
Kirkcaldy, February 2007

All the young men in the old photograph look pleased with themselves. They have pillbox hats and high-buttoned uniform jackets probably red or dark blue in colour, crossed diagonally with a sash. Their elbow-length gauntlets are white as also are their tight riding breeches, with black knee-length boots. They are grouped around a wooden table, bare but for steins of beer. Here an arm is cocked confidently on hip, there a fist rests commandingly on the table. Among those standing at the back one holds a tall banner. At the edge of the picture can be seen part of a large barrel, undoubtedly of beer. For all the world like a troop of Ruritanian Dragoons taking time off from guarding Princess Flavia to impress rustics at some wayside Inn. Karl Barth is the one sitting next to the beer barrel.

These were Berne members of Zofingia, a Swiss Student Association of which Barth was an enthusiastic member. Late in life he recalled how, as soon as he joined Zofingia he pranced proudly up and down the streets of Berne wearing its uniform cap. There was a serious side to Zofingia and in one of its debates in 1906 he pointed out that in Switzerland the gap between rich and poor between capital and labour was growing. These were issues with which Zofingia should be concerned and as a start he proposed the scrapping of those class distinctions which discouraged less well-off students from joining the Association. One of those who opposed Barth during this debate later became Minister of Justice and during the Second World War was to order the illegal tapping of Barth's telephone.

Both of Karl Barth's grandfathers had been pastors as had his father and the family into which he was born in 1886 in Basle was part of a secure and cultured elite within Swiss society. His intention was to become a pastor and though his University studies began in Switzerland he soon moved to Germany. For nearly a century Germany had been the unquestioned centre of a liberal and enlightened approach to religious ideas and this was what attracted Barth.

Throughout the 18th Century the claims of Christianity had grown ever more questionable. The increasing application of reason, of common sense even, to the reading of the Bible revealed contradictions and inconsistencies. Educated

Europeans were also becoming aware of other religions besides Christianity; not only Judaism, Islam, but also Buddhism and the other religions and philosophies of the East. At the end of the 18th Century one man in Germany feared that the coming age, with growing numbers of people becoming educated to think for themselves, would see education and intelligence on the one side and Christian faith and ignorance on the other.

"This is my vocation, to represent more clearly that which dwells in all true human beings, and to bring it home to their consciences". Beginning in 1799 with his "Speeches on Religion to its Cultured Despisers", Friedrich Schleiermacher worked, with romantic language and austere logic, to free Christian faith from becoming identified with ignorance. He explained to the cultured despisers of religion that doctrines, dogmas and propositions are not the essence of Christianity. They are inevitably flawed attempts to put into words and concepts the insights and intuitions of a religious awareness which is part of our deepest nature. "True religion is a sense and taste for the infinite" and "immediate consciousness of the Deity as he is found in ourselves and the world". All religions, Christianity included, are expressions of this consciousness of the divine, shaped and constrained by the cultures and environments within which they arise. The Bible, for example, is not some kind of infallible history book but the expression, in the culture of the time, of many such religious experiences. In Jesus Christ this consciousness of the divine reached its highest level. Theology should now be pursued as the attempt to understand religious experience, to understand what it means to be truly human, and also thereby to aid the creation of a more humane society. Schleiermacher bequeathed a huge and ambitious project. On the day after his death a colleague said: "From him, a new period in the history of the Church will one day take its origin". This is the period of modern liberal theology.

Barth studied first in Berlin, that city where more uniforms thronged the streets than anywhere else in Europe. Over 30 years before, on a fine morning in June 1871, Kaiser Wilhelm I rode at the head of a great procession from the Brandenburg Gate to the Palace, to take possession of Berlin as capital of a new Greater Germany, the new Reich. The glittering cavalcade took five hours to pass, there were masses of flags and flowers, great banners hung between the lime trees, and all the way to the Palace the route was lined with captured French guns. For a while the political life of this new capital had been dominated by regulations which outlawed any hint of Socialism. Now however the Social Democrats were growing in strength, marches and rallies were becoming more frequent and protesters and police clashed in the streets.

Barth was interested in none of this, so intense his absorption in theological studies. To be a student at that time at the Faculty of Theology of the University of Berlin was to have a unique opportunity to learn from the foremost Protestant historian of Christianity. Adolf Von Harnack was an aristocrat of intellect as well as by birth. With unflinching regard for strict historical truth, he brought the most rigorous of modern historical research techniques to study the development of early Christianity. Amidst the intellectual conflicts of the time, he ensured a hearing for the continuing relevance of Christianity. So great was Harnack's prestige, the demand for his books so huge, that when his 'What is Christianity' was published in 1899 freight trains full of copies blocked the railway station at Leipzig.

In one break from his studies Barth did get a fleeting glimpse of the wider city beyond, catching sight of the Kaiser and the King of Denmark riding past in state to the salutes of glittering guardsmen and it seemed to him like a picture out of some fairytale of long ago.

Others coming to Berlin for the first time found it devoid of any charm whatsoever. The young Rosa Luxemburg, visiting for the first time the city she would later try to seize and in which she would be murdered, found it cold and ugly, like a barracks. She longed for the sunshine: "You have no idea what darkness there is in Berlin during the winter". As for the Prussian ruling class their arrogant behaviour was "as if each one of them had been made to swallow the very stick with which he had got his daily beating."

From Berlin he moved to Marburg where the greatest impression on him was made by Wilhelm Herrmann, his tutor there from 1908. Long after much had come between them Barth could still say of Herrmann "even his physical appearance was wholly lacking in that trait of worldly wisdom and cunning which too often makes a systematic theologian recognisable, even at a distance". Herrmann's theology was firmly based upon the insights of Schleiermacher. Our faith is the arousal of our innate moral sense through contact with the life and teaching of Jesus. In this way we are able to grow in consciousness of God and of how to live.

Studying under such tutors Barth came to know that he could lead no better or more useful life than in developing and applying this modern liberal theology. It was not perfect, far from it, but it was the best which Christianity had yet produced.

In September 1909 he became assistant minister to the German-speaking Reformed Church in Geneva. His understanding of the ministry is clear from his very first sermon: "To be good friends, pathfinders, leaders in the sphere of inner life … we cannot do more. The time has gone forever when pastors wanted to be seen, and were seen, not only as messengers, but also as governors. We pastors and theologians have neither to administer nor to distribute religion: our task is always only to arouse, to encourage and to shape". His congregation were urged to be true to themselves, to become valuable, to know themselves as "before I can know God, I must know myself". He explained that Christian faith does not depend upon a series of external facts which have been handed down to us. It is dependent on the personal, inner life of Jesus and our response. The 17th Century poet Angelus Silesius was quoted:

"Were Christ a thousand times to Bethlehem come
And yet not born in thee, t'would spell thy doom
Golgotha's cross, it cannot save from sin
Except for thee that cross be raised within
I say, it helps thee not that Christ has risen
If thou thyself are still in death's dark prison".

Hard men had stood there before him, there in Geneva. This was Calvin's very pulpit and John Knox had also preached there. Calvin, who unveiled in the logic and lucidity of his theology a mirror in which can be glimpsed the inscrutable will of an infinite and eternal God. A will which, before the beginning of time, has predestined each and every one of us. As we take all the steps of our life, though every step may be freely chosen, we trace out in time the immutable pattern which has been chosen for us from all eternity.

At that time Barth saw no irreconcilable difference between such thinking of Calvin and the path he was now following. Modern theology is surely capable of integrating the most valuable of the insights of the past with the results of our increased knowledge and experience. What is of value in Calvin would be rescued from the restricted outlook of the times in which he lived and reinterpreted in the light of today. In those early days, ministering and preaching in Geneva, Barth was confident both in his work and of the future. There was however one distraction. As he worked into the gathering darkness of the night, preparing his sermons in his fourth floor flat, he could see and hear from the window a roller coaster which had been built below upon an island in the river Rhone. The roller coaster had lots of lights, a Swiss flag on top, and children of all ages swooped up and down to selections from "The Merry Widow".

CHAPTER 2

On the luminous morning of August 4 1914 seemingly endless columns of German troops invaded neutral Belgium. As they marched they sang. Their uniforms were grey and their belt-buckles bore the words "Gott mit uns". Neutral Belgium had been invaded so as to outflank the French frontier defences. Speed of advance was essential and any attempt by the Belgians to defend their country swiftly overcome. When the modern forts surrounding Liege refused to surrender, they were cracked open and their garrisons blown to bits by specially prepared giant siege guns. The civilian population was dealt with by an equal ruthlessness. The responses to any sign, or hint, of civilian resistance were appalling and extravagant reprisals.

The town of Andenne was burned to the ground and over a hundred and ten civilians shot. At Seilles, fifty were shot and houses looted and burned. At Tamines nearly four hundred were shot or bayoneted; at Dinant over six hundred, men and women both. There was no secrecy about these atrocities as they were intended to intimidate the civilian population as a whole.

The medieval city of Louvain was famous for its university, its unique library and its architectural and artistic treasures. After dark on 25 August some shots were fired. Who fired remained unclear but Louvain was punished in any event. The punishment lasted six days. When members of neutral legations eventually got through they found a ravaged city with dead bodies lying in the streets between the burning buildings. As news of Louvain swept around the world outrage grew in neutral countries, particularly America. Such criticism proved too much for the world of German culture, scholarship and religion. Ninety-three leading intellectuals issued a manifesto "To the Civilised World" supporting the Kaiser's war aims and pointing out the necessity of Germany's civilising mission. "It is not true" the manifesto proclaimed "that we have criminally violated the neutrality of Belgium... It is not true that our troops have brutally destroyed Louvain". Among the signatories were nearly all of Barth's German teachers, including Wilhelm Herrmann and Adolf Von Harnack, Director General of the Royal Library and Professor of Church History in Berlin.

Since July 1911 Karl Barth had been the pastor of the village of Safenwil in the Aargau in Switzerland. The church stood on some rising ground and a path led up to it from the rather damp parsonage below. Up this path Barth would go to deliver his Sunday sermon, to lead a funeral procession or to accompany his confirmation classes. Even, he reflected, behind the dung-cart. In his inaugural sermon the congregation were told "I am not speaking to you of God because I am a pastor. I am a pastor because I *must* speak to you of God if I am to remain true to myself, my better self". In the early years his sermons were often about the religious ideas of life and experience. His sermons were criticised for being too long and his funeral services for being too short. Church attendance was sparse and at times he felt that he and the people of Safenwil were staring at each other from opposite sides of a pane of glass.

Safenwil was changing in those years, an entire phase of European development and discontent reflected in a small Swiss village. A new school had just been built and electricity arrived by the end of 1913. Employment was changing from rural to predominantly industrial, concentrated in the weaving mill, dye-works and sawmill owned by the Hüssey family and the knitting mill of Herr Hochuli. Wages were low and the workers were not organised in Trade Unions. "Class warfare, which was going on in my parish before my very eyes, introduced me almost for the first time to the real problems of real life". Theology now took second place to the study of factory legislation, insurance, trade union affairs, economics and the reading of periodicals such as the "Textile Worker". In the evenings he set up adult education courses for men and women factory workers where he discussed with them such questions as work schedules and domestic finances. Most crucial and controversial, were his efforts in helping the Safenwil workers organise trade unions in face of opposition from the factory owners. For many he was now the 'Red Pastor.'

In December 1911 his theological and practical concerns came together in a lecture entitled "Jesus Christ and the Social Movement". "What Jesus brings to us are not ideas but a way of life. It is possible to have the most Christian ideas about God and the world, about man and his salvation, and yet, despite all this, still be a thoroughgoing pagan. And one can be a true follower and disciple of Christ and be an atheist, a materialist and a Darwinist". The nearly two thousand-year failure of the Christian church to deal with social needs was then contrasted with Jesus Christ as the "partisan of the poor". Socialism was not only the most urgent word of God to the present world but a continuation of the spiritual power which entered into history and life with Jesus. The use of material goods for self-seeking purposes was what Jesus had condemned as "unrighteous Mammon". Material goods should be held in service of the common good. While present day socialists had infinitely much to learn from Jesus, both the socialists and Jesus have the same goal "*Real* socialism is real Christianity in our time". Barth was, in effect, claiming Jesus Christ to be the first Socialist. He was, in time, to be confronted by people who claimed, with equal sincerity, that Jesus Christ was the first National Socialist.

Nelly Hoffman was not yet 18 when she became engaged to Barth in 1911. The youngest of five sisters she had been brought up entirely by her mother as her father, a lawyer and town clerk, died the year after she was born. Her mother moved the family to Geneva so that her children could have a good education, particularly in languages and art. Nelly Hoffman was studying the violin at the Conservatory and met Barth through the confirmation classes he gave in Geneva at that time. On becoming engaged she gave up her studies, spending some time in England during 1912 as a governess. They married in March 1913. A few months later Barth set out his views on marriage in a letter to a friend.

"With its gentle pressure, marriage sets to work on so many of the bristly features which are man's by nature, and helps to suppress them... Moreover, one is stimulated and helped in all kinds of good things: a wife gives loving criticism of sermons and speeches and is a spur to academic work; she is an extension of one's own work, looking after the girl's post-confirmation evenings, the mission classes and so on".

There is a temptation to invest this with significance in the light of later events. Nelly Barth is spoken of here only in terms of his work. When, years later, he persuaded Nelly to accept another woman into his life and house he was to justify this on the grounds that she too was essential for his work.

The events of August 1914 exposed more than one of the illusions of the time. Two years earlier Barth had attended a meeting of the Socialist International in Basel Cathedral in which war had been declared on war. By acting together socialists, in particular the Social Democratic parties of Germany and France could offer effective resistance to any declarations of war. Such aspirations did not appear unreasonable. That same year, one example among many, over 200,000 people attended an anti-war rally in Treptow Park in Berlin. During a controversy in July 1914 with a German theologian on the nature of socialism, a newspaper article by Barth poured scorn on any suggestion that the German Social Democratic Party was abandoning its revolutionary stance and becoming part of the established order. Hardly had the ink dried on Barth's article when the Kaiser appeared on the balcony of the Palace in Berlin to declare: "We are being forced to defend ourselves; the sword is being pressed into our hands. I urge you to go to church, to kneel before God, and plead with him to aid our courageous army." The Kaiser's speech had been written for him by Von Harnack. On the following day the German army marched into neutral Belgium and the Reichstag deputies of the Social Democratic Party listened to the Kaiser proclaim "We draw the sword with a clear conscience" and "From this day on I recognise no parties, only Germans". The Social Democrat deputies then joined enthusiastically in the cheers and shouts and unanimously voted the war credits required by the Kaiser for him to prosecute the war.

It was not only Barth whose expectations were cruelly confounded. The most acclaimed and influential British book of 1910 proved that the globalisation of trade and finance made war between developed nations such as Britain and Germany impossible. With irrefutable logic it demonstrated how in the economic interdependence of such nations the victor would suffer equally with the vanquished. As war would be ruinous to both sides no nation would be so self-destructive as to start one. So compelling were the book's arguments that study groups were formed in Universities. At the highest levels of the British Government it was claimed this book had shown that "a twentieth century war would be on such a scale that the inevitable consequences of commercial disaster, financial ruin and individual suffering were such as to make war unthinkable." The book's title was 'The Great Illusion.'

Barth later maintained that the 1914 manifesto of the ninety-three leading German intellectuals brought about his breech with the theological path he had followed so contentedly until then. His German teachers had taught him the unconditional truths of the Gospel and what it meant to perceive God in the life of the historical Jesus. Now Barth was being asked by them to accept something further. To accept that they perceived and experienced the war as a holy one, possessing religious significance as a fight by Germany for fundamental Christian values.

From pulpits all over Europe, Christianity was being put into the service of war. For Barth this was only to be expected; it was what usually happened. But the modern liberal theology he had been taught in Germany should have proved different. Instead, as he wrote to a friend: "The unconditional truths of the Gospel are simply suspended for the time being and in the meantime a German war-theology is put to work, it's Christian trimming consisting of a lot of talk about sacrifice and the like. Here is sufficient proof that the "truths" were nothing more than a surface varnish and not an innermost possession... it is truly sad".

Throughout Europe the Christian churches were giving spiritual support to the contending powers. The following is from a sermon preached in Scotland about those, our boys they are called, who volunteered for the British Army at the beginning of the war. Only the word "Teutonic" identifies from which side of the front line it was preached.

"We have witnessed in blood and fire and desolation the tragedy of the perceived ideal. Our boys have seen, as the whole world has seen, a working model of that foul idol of Teutonic political philosophy, the state as immorality organised; the State plus the resources of the chemist and the engineer but minus a conscience; the State with Christ and the ideals of Christ deliberately and even scornfully, as from some height of superior wisdom, ruled out from the sphere of collective action. It has not been a beautiful spectacle, but it has done its work. The heathen have returned and, at sight, the boys have rediscovered Christ. If He goes down they are going down with Him. That is the meaning of the look on their faces and it is the meaning of the smile, behind a mist of tears, in the heart of their mothers".

This sermon was considered so effective it was, along with some others, published in a book entitled "The Beautiful Thing That Has Happened To Our Boys".

Barth had a companion in perplexity. Eduard Thurneysen had become pastor of Leutwil about eight miles to the east of Safenwil in the summer of 1913. On the day of Thurneysen's inauguration Barth walked to Leutwil over the high ridges and valleys that separated the two villages. This was a journey each was to make many times. The two pastors continually visited each other to discuss how best to preach, how they could preach at all. To and fro they tramped, carrying their concerns and questions over the intervening ridges and through the valleys, but they were young and therefore confident, a time in life to be recalled wistfully in later years. "How good were those years when the great significance of all `our' insights, or lack of insights, manifested themselves only in our hurried walking back and forth on the Friesenweg and ... at most only the inhabitants of the villages of Holziken and Schöftland could shake their heads at the sight on the street of two strange wanderers between two worlds".

In 1915 Barth joined the Swiss socialists, the Swiss Social Democratic Party. This was a rare and bold move for a pastor in a Switzerland gripped by fear of socialist agitators stirring unrest, where workers worked twelve hour working days, where child labour was widespread, where restrictions were introduced on the right of public assembly and the army sent into Zurich when strikes were called. During an earlier much less sensitive period, a prominent minister had been forced by the church authorities to give up the title of minister when he joined the Social Democratic Party. Barth explained to Thurneysen "I have now become a member of the Social Democratic Party. Precisely because I am trying Sunday by Sunday to speak about last things, I could no longer allow myself to personally float in the clouds above the present evil world, rather it had to be demonstrated right now that faith in the Greatest does not exclude but rather includes work and suffering in a realm which is not yet complete."

That year the offensives stalled on the Western Front. On 25 September it was the turn of the British and Field Marshall Haig wrote in his diary "The greatest battle in the world's history begins today". Even with the use of poison gas his attack failed. The autumn offensive petered out after hundreds of thousands of casualties. That year the Germans and Austrians launched their offensive to break the Russians. The Russian army did not break, not that year, but after the offensive among the lakes and forests and marshes of the Eastern Front there were two million Russian casualties.

The United States of America would be next to enter the war against Germany. As in Europe there were many Christians who experienced a spiritual dimension in this call to arms. In the words of one influential preacher: "It is God who has summoned us to this war... This conflict is indeed a Crusade. The greatest in history - the holiest. It is in the profoundest and truest sense a Holy War... Yes it is Christ, the King of Righteousness who calls us to grapple in deadly strife with this unholy and blasphemous power". The more squeamish among American soldiers were encouraged by the Evangelical director of the American YMCA who said that he could picture Jesus Christ bayoneting Germans.

The Swiss authorities had just cause to be alarmed when they looked across the border at the growing social unrest in Germany. In 1915 Rosa Luxemburg, now one of the most radical leaders of the Social Democrats recorded the mood in Berlin. "The scene has fundamentally changed. Gone is the ecstasy and gone are the patriotic street demonstrations.....No more do trains filled with reservists pull out amid joyous cries from enthusiastic maidens. No longer do we see laughing faces smiling from train windows". Bread, potatoes, lard, eggs and milk and clothes were now rationed, coffee, tea and tobacco becoming harder and harder to obtain. The poor, now increasingly hungry as well, began to break into shops. On 1 May 1916 Rosa Luxemburg and her colleague Karl Liebknecht held a rally at the Potsdamer-Platz in Berlin, urging a crowd of several thousands to overthrow the Kaiser and his Government and end the war. When she was arrested for her activities there were widespread strikes and 50,000 workers demonstrated outside the Berlin courthouse where she was put on trial.

There were times when Barth felt like a bee, buzzing against a closed window, like someone blowing into a trumpet, cheeks puffed out but no sound emerging. In fact, there was a certain note beginning to emerge at that time, the note of what was to become his own distinctive voice. He was about to make a new beginning in theology and though this theology was to develop in detail, still unfolding even at his death fifty years later, much of it was there in that beginning. In reading him one has a sense that he became himself at that time and thereafter never ceased becoming ever more like himself.

In January 1916 he gave an address in the Town Church in Aarau. His audience were invited to contemplate the benefits of Christianity.

"It is a wonderful illusion, if we can comfort ourselves with it, that in our Europe... the Church's preaching, the Church's morality and the `religious life' go their uninterrupted way... A wonderful illusion, but an illusion, a self-deception. We should above all be honest and ask ourselves far more frankly what we really gain from religion. What is the use of all the preaching, baptising, confirming, bell-ringing and organ-playing of all the religious moods and modes... and whatever else may belong to this equipment of modern ecclesiasticism? Will something different eventuate from all this in our relation to the righteousness of God? Are we even expecting something different from it? Are we hoping that something may happen? Are we not rather hoping, by our very activity, to conceal in the most subtle way the fact that the critical event that ought to happen has not yet done so and probably never will?"

As for our God:

"He cannot prevent his worshippers, all the distinguished European and American apostles of civilisation, wealth and progress, all zealous citizens and pious Christians from falling upon one another with fire and sword to the amazement and derision of the poor heathen in India and Africa. This God is really an unrighteous God, and it is high time for us to declare ourselves thoroughgoing doubters, sceptics, scoffers and atheists in regard to him. It is high time for us to confess freely and gladly; this God to whom we have built the Tower of Babel is not God. He is an idol. He is dead".

CHAPTER 3

Many years later, when both were old and Barth was famous, Eduard Thurneysen wrote an Introduction to the publication of a selection from their early correspondence with each other. On the basis of their life-long friendship, Thurneysen considered that neither at Safenwil nor later was Barth ever an abstract or speculative thinker. For Thurneysen, Barth was and remained a man who tried to study the Bible and to tell of what he found there. Even so, he could not dispute that for Barth the nature of the Bible is not a simple matter but deeply problematic.

"What is there within the Bible? What is the significance of the remarkable line from Abraham to Christ? What of the chorus of Prophets and Apostles and what is the burden of their song? What is the one truth that these voices evidently all desire to announce, each in its own tone, each in its own way? What lies between the strange statement, In the beginning God created Heaven and Earth, and the equally strange cry of longing, Even so come, Lord Jesus! What is there behind all this, that labours for expression. ... Is it true, this talk of a loving and good God, who is more than one of the friendly idols whose rise it is so easy to account for and whose dominion is so brief? What the people want to find out and thoroughly understand is, is it true?... They want to find out and thoroughly understand: they do not want to hear mere assertions and asseverations, however fervent and enthusiastic they may be. And they want to find out and thoroughly understand the answer to this one question "is it true"". As the pupil of Von Harnack, as the inheritor of the long tradition of German scholarly biblical research, Barth did not dispute in any way the necessity of applying such research and being willing to learn from its results. He regarded the scholarly and critical approach as an essential preliminary, but if in doing that alone we think that we are interpreting the Bible we have in fact stopped before actual understanding has even begun. Neither did he have any sympathy for biblical fundamentalism, regarding it as a typical product of rationalist thinking; by learning and repeating the words of the Bible we think we have grasped God and his revelation.

Barth did not find the contents of the Bible easy to understand, needing only to be put into contemporary language to become generally comprehensible. The ubiquitous admonition "to let the Bible speak" also turned out to be easier said than done. Instead, what he now found within the Bible was quite different, quite unexpected and strange. "When we come to the Bible with our questions - how shall I think of God and the universe? How arrive at the Divine? ... It answers us, as it were, "My Dear Sir, these are *your* problems: you must not ask *me*! Whether it is better to hear mass or hear a sermon, whether the proper form of Christianity is to be discovered in the Salvation Army or in Christian Science, whether the better belief is that of old Rev Dr Smith or young Rev Mr Jones, whether your religion should be more a religion of the understanding, of the will, or of the feelings, you can and must decide for yourself. If you do not care to enter upon *my* questions, you may, to be sure, find in me all sorts of arguments and quasi-arguments for one or another stand point, but you will not then find what is really here."

There was an unpleasant scene one afternoon in the villa of Herr Hochuli. The owner of the knitting mill and the pastor of Safenwil sit in deep easy chairs making polite talk. Fifty-five women employees at the knitting mill have organised themselves into a trade union and Herr Hochuli has threatened them with dismissal. Barth is pressing Herr Hochuli to change his mind. In a later, only partly self-mocking, description of this encounter he compares himself, somewhat tritely, to Moses asking Pharaoh Hochuli to free his workers from bondage. Politeness can only go so far. Hochuli's patience snapped and he called Barth the worst enemy he had ever had in his whole life.

Barth's speeches in support of the workers, his activities in the establishment of trade unions disturbed many among his congregation. When he was thought to have praised a general strike four of the six members of his church committee resigned in protest. A May Day parade in which he walked with the Safenwil workers behind the Red Flag provoked many to join Herr Hochuli in leaving the church and to take part in a "worship association" set up by the mill owner.

In an address which he gave in Thurneysen's church at Leutwil in the autumn of 1916 Barth outlined some of the matters he did not find in the Bible. This was still a time of necessary negations, of clearing away.

"At certain crucial points the Bible amazes us by its remarkable indifference to our conception of good and evil.

Abraham, for instance, as the highest proof of his faith, desires to sacrifice his son to God. Jacob wins the birthright by a refined deception of his blind father; Elijah slays the four hundred and fifty priests of Baal by the brook Kishon. Are these exactly praiseworthy examples?

And in how many phases of morality the Bible is grievously wanting! How little fundamental information it offers in regard to the difficult questions of business life, marriage, civilisation and statecraft, with which we have to struggle! To mention only a single problem, but to us today a mortal one; how unceremoniously and constantly war is waged in the Bible. Time and again, when this question comes up, the teacher or minister must resort to various kinds of extra-biblical material because the New as well as the Old Testament always completely breaks down at this point. Time and again serious Christian people who seek "comfort" and "inspiration" in the midst of personal difficulties will quietly close their Bibles and reach for the clearer-toned lyre of a Christian Füchtegott Gellert... if not towards psycho-analysis - where everything is so much more practicable, simple and comprehensible. Time and again the Bible gives us the impression that it contains no instructions, counsels or examples, whatsoever, either for individuals or for nations and governments; and the impression is correct. It offers us not at all what we first seek in it."

There arrived a well-known preacher for a week of evangelism. To Barth it was like an artillery barrage being rolled back and forth over Safenwil. At one point he crept out of his trench to report on the work of evangelism to Thurneysen: "Last night he really let himself go: It was very bloody and went very badly with the human race. We listened very patiently, anxious about what is yet to come". He listened to a gospel of our salvation which proceeds by way of awakenings, conversions, sealings, and different levels of resistance to the Holy Spirit with Christ's blood flowing as medicine for the soul. Even so "continually there were the open jaws of Hell into which a man could disappear in spite of all these splendours". On Sunday, when the week of evangelism had come to an end Barth retook his pulpit and "in contrast to all the soul experiences and gruesome thundering about sin" preached to his flock that there is joy with God and that the Kingdom of God on earth begins with joy.

In Germany the Social Democratic Party was itself disintegrating. The moderates, cautious and reformist, were confident that they would soon gain power by democratic means. Yet another delusion said the radicals and, led by Rosa Luxemburg and Karl Liebknecht, broke away to form a new Party, the Spartacus Alliance. When the already small bread ration was halved 300,000 members of the metal workers union went on strike and marched through the streets of Berlin. The Kaiser and the High Command were now saying that the real enemies of Germany were not those on the Eastern and Western Fronts but the agitators within.

As Barth worked and studied he questioned what the emphasis on "feeling" or "spiritual experience" had to do with the people in the Bible. He was now coming to believe that when, like Schleiermacher, we speak about religious feelings and experiences, we are not really talking about God but only about ourselves in a loud voice. "Can one", Barth asked his Leutwil audience, "read or hear read even as much as two chapters of the Bible and still with a good conscience say, God's word went forth to humanity. His mandate guided history from Abraham to Christ. The Holy Spirit descended in tongues of fire upon the Apostles at Pentecost, Saul became a Paul and travelled over land and sea - all in order that here and there specimens of men like you and me might be "converted", find inner "peace" and by a redeeming death go some day to "Heaven". Is *that* all? Is *that* all of God and his new world, of the meaning of the Bible, of the content of the contents... is not God - greater than that?"

As the butcher work of war dragged on the peoples of Europe were not to be deprived of the consolations of religion. To quote once more from "The Beautiful Thing That Has Happened To Our Boys".
"Think you there was no sacrifice, that they felt no pull of the dear things they left behind? Yet what peace it was, peace-passing understanding, to follow where duty called. What an uplift of the soul to give, deliberately to give all, up to the last ounce of energy. To yield, if need be, life itself in the service of things greater than life. Fathers and mothers and friends, whose hearts are with your dear ones in Flanders or where they stand two thousand miles away in Gallipoli fronting the unknown, you must not pity them. They are far beyond that. Yonder, where the flag of freedom flies and the blades of heroes fends it round, they are happy - these boys of ours - even amid all the dreadful things, for the glory and the joy of sacrifice is in their souls". 'Our boys' however were long

gone, thrown away. Late in his life Barth was to write about the specifically Christian form of falsehood, what he was to call the "Sunday lie".

Since 1914 there had been stalemate on the Western Front. With their numerical superiority the armies of the British and French Empires had launched offensive after offensive against the German lines. Though every offensive had failed to break through, and the withdrawal of Russia from the war had enabled the Western Front to be reinforced, time was running out for Germany. Hundreds of thousands of American troops were arriving in France, millions more were on their way. The allied blockade was finally strangling the German economy which in any event could not compete with the avalanche of shells, tanks, guns, and aeroplanes coming out of the factories of America, Britain and France. Essentials were growing ever more scarce. It was now or never.

In the early hours of the morning of March 21, 1918, a morning of fog, a brief but intense German artillery barrage was directed against that part of the Western Front held by the British Third and Fifth Armies. The barrage lifted and the German elite units, the storm troopers, rose out of their trenches and advanced across No-Man's-Land. Four years of stalemate were over. The British Fifth Army was shattered, the Third Army pushed back and the Germans were once more, as in those far-off days of August 1914, marching towards Paris.

Barth concluded that if a new beginning had to be made in theology, and it had, he would have to make it himself. So he turned to Paul's "Epistle to the Romans", that text where both Greek and Jew are shown to be equally without excuse, where there is no just man, and where justification is solely through faith in the God who raises Jesus from the dead. A text central and crucial to Protestant theology. He applied himself to "Romans" with all the resources he then had at his disposal, reading as if he had never read it before, noting down what he discovered point by point, reading and reading, day by day for weeks and then months. He began in a garden, sitting under an apple tree; it is unlikely that the irony was totally lost on him. After a while he reported: "During the work it is often as though I were being looked at by something from afar, from Asia Minor or Corinth, something very ancient, early oriental, indefinably sunny, wild, original, that somehow is hidden behind these sentences and is so ready to let itself be drawn forth by ever new generations..."

The first edition of Barth's commentary on Paul, his 'Romerbrief' was published towards the end of 1918. Three weeks earlier the Kaiser had left his Palace for the last time, driving down Unter den Linden and through the Brandenburg Gate, reversing the route taken by his father when coming to claim Berlin as capital of the new Reich. There were only sparse crowds in the streets to see him depart for his military headquarters at Spa in Belgium, streets described by the painter George Grosz: "the houses were cracked, paint and plaster had crumbled away, and in the dull eye-sockets of the windows you could see the caked traces of tears; the tears of people that were looking for familiar faces that were never to return."

The gamble of the March offensive had failed, Paris had not fallen. Now the Navy had mutinied and a mass peace movement was sweeping Germany. On the afternoon of Saturday 9th November there was utter confusion in the corridors of the Reichstag while a huge crowd milled in uncertainty outside. Armed deserters lounged in the corridors while in the restaurant on the second floor the Social Democratic deputy Philip Scheidemann was trying to find something to eat when he was approached and urged to say something to the increasingly restive crowd outside. Opening a window he leaned out and shouted down: "The old and the rotten have broken down. Long live the new! Long live the German Republic".

Thus were the Kaiser and the Second Reich overthrown in what came to be called the Revolution of November 1918. The Social Democrat leaders of the new Republic agreed to an armistice with Germany's enemies and two days later the Great War was over.

Germany was about to undergo a cruel peace. Amongst the works written at that time was Ernst Jünger's "Storm of Steel". One time captain of storm troopers, holder of his country's highest awards for bravery, he ended his book with a call to his generation, those just old enough to have experienced with him the life of the front-line. He speaks of those last battles, and then: "Now these too are over, and already we see once more in the dim light of the future the tumult of fresh ones. We - by this I mean those of the youth of this land who are capable of enthusiasm for an ideal - will not shrink from them. We stand in the memory of the dead who are holy to us, and we believe ourselves entrusted with the true and spiritual welfare of our people. We stand for what will be and for what has been. Though force without and barbarity within conglomerate in sombre clouds, yet so long as the blade of a sword will strike a spark in the night may it be said: Germany lives and Germany shall never go under!"

The first edition of Barth's "Römerbrief" proved a moderate, academic success. On the basis of that first edition, he received, early in 1921, an invitation to take up a new chair of Reformed Theology to be established later that year in Germany at Göttingen. Even before that invitation he had begun to revise the "Römerbrief". He now felt the first edition to be too speculative and that he could say what had to be said in a much clearer and effective manner. To say the same thing in a different way.

The second edition of "Römerbrief" did not bring moderate success. Instead it brought fame and notoriety, dedicated followers and the bitter tribute of passionate opposition. While written in Safenwil it was not published until early 1922 by which time Barth had taken up his new post in Germany. There is justice in this. While the matters with which the book deals are common to all times, and Barth certainly had no intention of writing only in or to the spirit of the times, this second "Römerbrief" like certain works of art seems by some inexplicable alchemy to capture and embody the essence of a particular time and place. Not the problems and aspirations of a small town in Switzerland but the extremes, the intoxicating nihilism and dangerous glamour of Weimar Germany with its sense of total crisis and the necessity of a radical new beginning.

He was all too conscious of his failures as pastor of Safenwil though he took some comfort in leaving behind three flourishing trade unions. Late in 1921, Karl and Nelly Barth and their four children set off for Göttingen. On his departure he wrote to Thurneysen, "It may well be that we shall soon look back on the trouble and turmoil and wearisome labour of this time as one looks back upon a happy boyhood. What is to come may be the heat of the summer." A more portentous metaphor suggested itself to Thurneysen who was himself working on a study of Dostoevsky. In pursuing their new course in theology he pictured Barth and himself as on a polar expedition, destination unknown. In leaving for Germany Barth was breaking off on his own to follow a trail into the further distance, the ever further north, into the heart of the inland ice.

Two months after his arrival in the Winter Kingdom, Barth received a Doctorate in Theology. His eight-year-old daughter asked whether that meant he was now able to make little children well.

CHAPTER 4

At Göttingen, Barth was greeted with outward civility and scarcely concealed hostility. This hostility was due in large part to Göttingen being a Lutheran stronghold. There were those who looked upon the new post in Reformed Theology, of the tradition of Calvin rather than Luther, as demeaning the faculty. Initial hostility did not diminish with increasing acquaintance. Barth's growing fame and influence within the wider world of German theology did not help matters. Neither did the increasing number of Lutheran students who attended his lectures when they should have been attending Lutheran lectures delivered by Lutheran lecturers.

The students were an unusual group in themselves. Many were war veterans, including a company commander, an artillery battery commander and an ex-lieutenant of the Austrian Imperial Guard who now laid paving in the street for several hours each day in order to eat.

Power slipped away from the Social Democrats even as they grasped it. As they hastened to sign the Armistice the leadership, cautious constitutionalists and solid trade unionists as they were, had a vision of a return to peace followed by a programme of moderate social reform. Long denounced as dangerous agitators they were now in turn rejected as hopeless reactionaries by that great peace movement which had engulfed the Reich and which now demanded instant and revolutionary social changes. On New Year's Eve 1919 the radical wing of the Party, the Independent Social Democrats merged with the Spartacus Alliance to form the Communist Party of Germany under the leadership of Rosa Luxemburg and Karl Liebknecht. From the very balcony of the Palace from which they had been denounced by the Kaiser, the Social Democrats were now denounced as leftovers from the old order. In a tumult of revolutionary demands, armed workers and soldiers councils took over one after the other of Germany's major cities.

Hopes that the army, now returning from the Front, would restore law and order, dissolved with the army itself as the soldiers simply kept on walking back to their homes. Many thousands however kept their weapons and joined the swelling ranks of the communists. Quite separately, a handful of former storm troopers, unable to accept either defeat or civilian life occupied part of an abandoned army camp on the outskirts of Berlin, swearing allegiance only to their former officers. These were the first of the Freicorps, their contempt for the Social Democrat government exceeded only by that for the huge and growing army of communists.

In a harsh winter while thousands died from hunger and influenza the streets of Berlin were filled increasingly with crowds of armed revolutionaries and the Red Flag was hoisted from government buildings and even from the top of the Brandenburg Gate itself. The government could only look on helplessly as the communists took over Berlin. Then in the space of a few days it was all over, the communists shattered and in flight, their two leaders murdered. The Freicorps had come to the aid of the despised Social Democrats. The Great War was over, the Weimar Republic was about to come into being, but Germany was far from being at peace.

To the Protestant Church in Germany, to Lutherans and Reformed alike, defeat in the Great War brought a particular bitterness and despair. This was a church which regarded itself as the church of the "German" Reformation, a church both nationalist and monarchist. Religion was a matter of loyalty to throne and altar. Now the Kaiser had fled, his Reich dissolved and a godless republic installed in its place. When church delegates from all over Germany met in Dresden in 1919, the opening address spoke for them all: "The glory of the German Imperial Reich, the dream of our fathers, the pride of every German is gone, with it have gone those lofty figures who supported German power, the ruler and the ruling house, whom we loved and honoured so deeply, as standard bearers of German greatness...... we can do nothing else here but bear solemn witness to what rich blessings have issued from the previous close relations between state and church upon both state and church, and through both these upon the people and the fatherland."

Defeat was all the more painful as German Protestantism in particular had identified the German cause with God's will, and the inevitable German victory as that of civilisation over barbarism, of German faith and piety over the numerically superior forces of materialism. Just so would God's will again be seen to be working in history. Defeat therefore was not only bitter, it was inexplicable, absurd. Immediately after the signing of the Peace Treaty, the editor of the Church's Year Book asked "Where is the justice of God? The question torments thousands, including those who long ago recognised and criticised the inner decline of her people, its mammonism, its passion for pleasure..... are the others any better? It not mammonism an import from America; and cold-hearted egoism England's dowry? And moral decline bound up with the insatiable virulence of France's vulgar style? Are we not seeing a triumph of lies and a success of vulgarity of a kind that was rare even in the darkest periods of history?"

Germany was stripped of her colonies and border territories, forced to admit sole responsibility for the war, forced to pay the war pensions of her enemies. With German industry and trade ruined after four years of war and blockade, her victorious enemies still demanded three quarters of her merchant fleet, a quarter of her fishing fleet, and thousands of locomotives and lorries. The Rhineland was occupied, with all the costs of occupation falling on the occupied. All this in addition to being forced to pay war reparations three times greater than she could hope to pay in the time given.

The results were increasing poverty, inflation, and unemployment. The clergy suffered along with the rest; in Brunswick the quarterly income of a pastor in the autumn of 1922 was less than the weekly wage of an unskilled labourer. Hardly surprising that Barth had doubts about the value of teaching theology in Germany at such a time. He wondered whether he should not throw all "theological rubbish" into a corner and become a social worker who could bring as many Swiss francs as possible into Germany for the various charity and relief organisations. He watched, almost breathlessly, as inflation soared and destroyed the value of money. "People hunger and freeze notoriously in their thousands: Tuberculosis and strange hunger diseases get the upper hand..... it is very bad". He wrote that in December 1922; the following month, as Germany fell behind in the payment of reparations, French troops occupied the Ruhr, seizing its factories, goods and raw materials. At this further shock and loss the German economy now entered un-chartered realms of madness. Before inflation peaked in late 1923 one American dollar bought four trillion, two hundred billion marks. Barth told Thurneysen that the French invasion of the Ruhr made even his Swiss blood boil. He now thought he was beginning to perceive things as a German would. Regardless of whoever may or may not have had "right" on their side, he believed a "fearful bowl of anger" was gathering and that sooner or later the Germans would march upon their enemies in the West "even though it should only be with scythes and flails".

In Berlin the wife of the British Ambassador recorded in her diary the life of the city as seen from her window. As early as four am underfed men and women, with drawn faces and bent shoulders passed below on their way to work with thin clothes and ill shod feet, returning only at dusk. As she wrote this entry she could see below a skeleton of a boy slowly dragging a cart full of miserable merchandise. Once, in winter, in the small back room of a basement flat she came upon a young woman and her six-year-old child. The woman was sitting on a deal box; there was no other furniture and no fire. Her husband had been a shoemaker but after he had gone to the war she had grown poorer and poorer and had to sell everything she had to get food. Now she was alone in this bleak and terrible room with her child clinging to her torn dress which she no longer had spirit or hope or needle and thread to mend.

The Ambassador's wife also recorded sights and events of a different nature. In October 1920 for example, at the first official party at the British Embassy after the War there were about 300 people in the white and yellow ballroom, with servants in buff and scarlet liveries and at the entrance two retainers in cocked hats and long gold-laced coats. The following month Princess Radziwill returned to Berlin to recover "some wonderful jewels" which had been kept for her in a Government safe, and threw a lavish dinner party at the Hotel Adlon. The month after that, also at the Hotel Adlon, a Benevolence Ball was held; the 1,500 of Berlin's wealthy who attended managed between them to hand over £1500 for the soup kitchens feeding the hungry. This was the same week as that in which the Ambassador's wife wrote: "It is a pretty sight to watch old-fashioned sleighs gliding smoothly and silently across the ice-blue Tiergarten ...the occupants often smothered in furs..."

Strange hunger dreams in Göttingen, drawn faces in Berlin and the rich in furs gliding over the ice. Works of theology can shrivel, become irrelevant, when read in the light cast by such a world. It was and remains a strength of Barth's second edition of "Römerbrief" that such a world is not alien to its vision. "Römerbrief" stands in its own very particular light in which that world is seen to be as natural as our own while our own world is seen to be equally surreal and desperate.

Even in the Preface, where methodology is discussed, there is a challenge to academic theology. "The historical critical method of biblical research has its place; it points to a preparation for understanding that is never superfluous. But if I had to choose between it and the old doctrine of inspiration, I would resolutely choose the latter. It has a greater, deeper, more important place because it points directly to the task of understanding, without which all preparation is worthless. I am happy that I do not have to choose between the two. But my entire attention has been directed toward looking *through* the historical to the spiritual dimension of the Bible, where we find the eternal Spirit. What was once a serious matter is still serious today."

To summarise "Römerbrief" is to render it flat and insipid, neutralising its offence. Also, no English translation can convey adequately the multiple layers of indirect allusion to German theology and philosophy contained in the original text. Such barriers are only just however in attempting to convey the flavour of a book which argues, among other matters, that theology is an impossible undertaking.

What Barth found in Paul's Epistle to the Romans was the otherness of God. God does not lie at the end of some human search, whether of Schleiermacher or any other. There is no way from us to God.

"All divinities which dwell on this side of the line of resurrection; no divinity which dwells in temples made with hands or which is served by the hand of a man; no divinity which *needs anything*, any human propaganda - can be God...... God the pure and absolute boundary and beginning of all that we are and have and do; God who is distinguished qualitatively from men and from everything human, and must never be identified with anything which we name, or experience, or conceive or worship as God...... he who says "God" says "miracle"..... We, however, are capable only of rejecting, denying, sleeping and misapprehending. We are incompetent to see what is invisible and to comprehend what is incomprehensible. We have no sensible organ wherewith to perceive the miracle."

It is impossible for us to talk of this God. Therefore theology is impossible. But this wholly other God of the Bible is the God who has come to us in Jesus Christ, therefore we must talk of God. Theology is this impossible possibility.

The style, method and concepts of "Römerbrief" attempt to embody this paradox. Affirmations are continuously negated by their opposites, statements spiral around each other cancelling each other out. The book attempts to let us see that what we need is impossible for us, but what is impossible for us is possible for God. "In the Gospel, in the message of salvation of Jesus Christ, this hidden, living God has revealed Himself as He is."

And so on for 500 wild and dizzy pages. Telling us that any God of whom direct talk is possible is not God and that any hope which is visible is not hope. Of our redemption which is invisible, inaccessible, impossible, yet which comes to us as hope. For some "Römerbrief" is simply unreadable; others find in it only noise and fury signifying little. To persevere in reading to the end requires a dedicated stamina. Barth himself came to be critical of some aspects of it. Even so it still retains a certain power to attract or repel. Even though they may only sample its pages, it is still possible that some readers may suddenly have the sensation that the walls separating our century from the first have grown thinner and that they can catch a genuine echo of a message originally sent two thousand years before.

"If then, we are to live in Pauline fashion, we must dare to live freely. Oppressed on all sides by God and wholly dissolved by him; reminded constantly of death and as constantly directed towards life; scared out of the petty trivialities of human relationships in which men are normally imprisoned and therefore free to apprehend what is certain and living and eternal; depending only upon the forgiveness of sins and therefore able to direct their conduct with real clarity of insight; our reverence for all relative values and factors so completely shattered that we are enabled to make genuine and proper use of them; so securely bound and chained to God that we can preserve a calm independence with regard to those many problems and requirements and duties of life which are not imposed upon us directly by God himself and by him only; loosed - or shall we say "relativised" in a negative and positive sense of the word - from the whole compulsion of authority and regimentation, from the whole multiplicity of god-like powers and authorities which make up our world - is not this the Pauline freedom and detachment?"

A few months before Barth's arrival in Göttingen, the Finance Minister of the Weimar Republic was murdered while walking in the Black Forest. A few months after his arrival, the Foreign Minister was murdered in Berlin by the same group of nationalist extremists. Walter Rathenau had been recognised throughout Europe as an original thinker, a brilliant politician, and a tireless worker for the good of his country. A leading capitalist, he had earned the respect of the notoriously left-wing Berlin trade unions, who announced a day of mourning for his death. When his body lay in state in the Parliament building, the Reichstag, a million Berliners paraded through the pouring rain in his honour. Not all Germans, however, were horrified by this murder. In Berlin, the students of Berlin University refused to pay their respects. In Göttingen, Barth listened to colleagues in the Theological Faculty condoning Rathenau's murder. After all, they explained, the German Government was no place for a Jew.

The Weimar Republic had few friends in such circles. During his years in Germany, Barth found that "with very few exceptions, the professors whom I came to know socially ... had what I can only describe as an attitude of sabotage towards the poor Weimar Republic". None more so than a brilliant fellow – theologian.

CHAPTER 5

"We stand in danger", said Emanuel Hirsch "of being brought low, of being destroyed as a people, so that only a formless mass of workers is left in the service of foreign interests. This status is so dreadful, so contradicts what we and no others could accomplish among humanity, that it constantly raises doubts about the meaning and justice of history".

Hirsch arrived in Göttingen at the same time as Barth. While Barth was a young professor, Hirsch was an even younger one. "A learned and acute man", Barth reported to Thurneysen, "A profound knowledge of Luther and Fichte an effete figure of a scholar of the kind to be found in books, German nationalist to his very fragile bones, but a notable phenomenon". That Hirsch made a decided impression, that his learning and undoubted brilliance unsettled Barth is evident under a coating of defensive irony. "This Hirsch really knows an awful lot. He expresses his opinion on Indian religious history, Islam, the relationships in inner Africa, old and new methods of missions, fairytale research, Homeric heroes, etc. with an expert knowledge which leaves me standing there with my mouth hanging open. I barely had heard the names of most of these things, and that is not even the speciality of this contortionist."

Hirsch believed that while we have an inner knowledge of eternal truth, Christianity will die if it refuses to re-think its message with changing times. While we have grown richer in knowledge of the things of the external world, we are poor in the knowledge of inner truths. Our rationalism is forever unsettling, never creative. While we grasp technical goals, we are unable to integrate our knowledge into patterns of a higher order. For the sake of truth itself, there comes a time when the intellectually active person must rebel and affirm creative, non-rational values, and seek in the contemplation of the Spirit guidelines for the life of the individual and society.

At Göttingen, Hirsch and Barth circled and prowled around each other, sometimes bristling, sometimes friendly, always interested, but always wary. Opposites in all but a grudging respect for each other's ability. At times Barth could be quite patronising. "It is hard enough for me to swallow his eccentricities, his Berlin ways and academic airs, but my ingredients are no less difficult to him..... if only some one of you could invite him to Switzerland for a couple of weeks in the summer; he works himself into the ground so pitifully and he should really be preserved for the church for some years yet. It would be a real comfort for me if I could see him again in some meadow eating milk and cheese. But Good Heavens, I could bring you a whole train-full of such Germans......"

Religion for Hirsch was a matter of the message of Jesus Christ acting upon our conscience. While God is to be heard in the "accusation and demand of the conscience", this conscience is not the individual conscience only, but also the conscience of the nation. In both the Bible and nature, to recognise that God has created me is to recognise that my nation and race are also the result of the creative will of God. Each nation, each race has its particular relationship to God and its particular mission to fulfil. For Germans to recover hope, to discover and carry out their particular mission, depended upon "becoming a pious People, a People among whom the gospel has power over the conscience".

Barth complained that Hirsch gave far too much importance to concepts such as "heart" and "conscience". As Hirsch's general conversation was filled with phrases like "war-guilt lie", "humiliating peace" and "enemy league", Barth suspected that such phrases revealed the situation which was really important to Hirsch and for which he searched the Bible to provide himself with a good "conscience".

At this time Barth had a number of exchanges with Adolf Von Harnack. Having devoted his life to bringing religion, science and culture together Von Harnack was disturbed to detect in his former pupil the return of an old heresy, an echo of Marcion. Von Harnack knew only too well the threat which Marcion had once posed to the early Christian church. On one side had stood what we now accept as Christianity, on the other stood Marcion and Christianity had survived only by the skin of its teeth.

Born on the northern shores of Anatolia in 85 AD Marcion saw in the Old Testament (and it is to Marcion that we owe the terms Old and New Testaments) only a history of crimes and massacres. He found there an uncaring and cruel universe, a corrupt world ruled by its creator, Jehovah the God of the Old Testament, a God obsessed with instilling fear so that he could compel worship. Then Jesus Christ had entered this impoverished and tormented world to reveal a totally strange God whose Son he was. This un-guessed-at God is the true

God, the God of a completely New Testament. The true God is the God of grace and love and mercy and Jesus Christ His Son came to teach us to love each other and turn away from Jehovah's world towards that other world which has been prepared for us as our new and true home. While Marcion was finally denounced as a heretic and forced to retire from the Church, there had been a moment when he had so many disciples that, in the words of an opponent, they seemed to "fill the whole universe". Even three centuries later Marcionite churches were still to be found in Rome, Egypt and Asia Minor.

This then was what Von Harnack saw in Barth, the return of an ancient danger. Their exchanges however led to no resolution and Von Harnack prophesied that Barth would end up by founding a sect.

Even earlier than Marcion there had been another yet similar threat to Christianity. Simon Magus is a figure from the pages of the Acts of the Apostles and the very earliest Christian writings. Even at the time when the Roman Empire teemed as never before with sages, miracle workers, assorted saviours and messiahs with their inevitable disciples, Simon Magus threw a unique shadow over the ambitions of the Apostles. He travelled the eastern roads of the Empire accompanied always by a woman called Helen, declaring that he was the Sun and she the Moon, he the Power and she the Wisdom. He too declared that Jehovah was a lesser god, a petty authoritarian demanding worship and imposing penalties. There is however a way to escape the prison Jehovah has created. Within each of us is a free divine spark, but it must be discovered and developed else it die with the body. We must therefore establish in our own lives the true order of things, the union of power and wisdom as symbolised in the union between himself and Helen.

Everywhere Simon Magus and Helen went they drew crowds, frustrating the work and teaching of the Apostles. Eventually, during a dispute in Rome itself, Peter challenges Simon Magus to demonstrate his powers by rising high into the sky. Simon does so whereupon Peter prays that Simon may fall which he does and is killed. The very earliest Christians who passed on this account of Simon's death doubted neither its veracity nor that it proved the moral and spiritual superiority of Christianity.

Whether or not Barth at this time had any theological resemblance to Marcion he was in fact to acquire a more personal resemblance to Simon Magus. His theological travels, both physically and intellectually, were soon to be carried out with a woman who was to add her own wisdom to his work.

In November 1924 Barth attended a service of dedication for a memorial to the seven hundred Göttingen students and professors who had fallen in the Great War. The old Field Marshall Von Hindenburg was one of the participants. In a report to his own circle Barth was less than impressed by the tone and content of most of the speeches. "Young heroes - August 1914 - German in the heart and on the lips - the individual must die that the state may live - they have entered Valhalla - they live eternally in our hearts - shameful peace of Versailles - November men of 1918 - true to the death - better times - when the next war comes - property and life - what young German hearts would not - German oakwoods - victor in a thousand battles - fallen heroes - you too will." Then Hindenburg, leaning on his sword, began to speak. His words were few but measured and it seemed to Barth as if the old Field Marshall spoke with a lion's voice and that, as he spoke, the very birds of the trees fell silent.

Barth also recorded his impressions of formal celebrations in an ardently nationalist student fraternity. The only matters it had in common with the student beer drinking with which he was familiar were students and beer. "Otherwise everything is different. Dreadfully stiff, ordered, well behaved, polished, rigidly national. Everything that might disturb the illusion is kept at a distance. Instead there are songs such as "God lets the iron grow......" in which the shedding of "French blood" shortly is contemplated. And at the end, a tiresome cultic act: "To the fathers of the nation" with the endless rattling of swords and the singing of the same words and the same tune one hundred and fifty times. The extent to which they give themselves up to illusions is quite unbelievable".

"We are the authors of our own fate", wrote Emanuel Hirsch referring to the catastrophe of defeat, occupation and economic collapse. Others came to different conclusions. Field Marshall Erich Ludendorff, Chief of Operations in the Great War and second only to Hindenberg in popularity as a military commander, led the readers of his memoirs into the very inner sanctum of the deliberations of the High Command. They could now learn for the first time of how, in his efforts to save his People, Ludendorff had become aware of something secret and mysterious working against him. Of how, penetrating ever more deeply into the conditions which brought about defeat and calamity (a defeat and calamity not, of course, to be laid in any way at the door of the High Command), he had discovered ever more secret and supra-national forces which had worked to destroy the will of the People. Namely "the Jewish race and Rome along with their tools, the Freemasons, the Jesuits and occult and satanic groups."

Another ex-soldier, though he had been only a corporal was far more focused and decisive than Ludendorff when describing his own particular moment of truth. In his account of his struggle he tells of how he learns of the defeat while lying in a military hospital temporarily blinded after a gas attack. The shame of defeat and disgrace burns into him; what is the pain in his eyes compared to this misery. Days of torment are followed by nights which are even more terrible and in the nights hate grows; hate for those responsible. Then, in that melodramatic style which his followers were also to adopt, he says:

"There is no making pacts with Jews; there can only be the hard either-or.
I for my part, decided to go into politics".

CHAPTER 6

George Mertz was a Lutheran pastor and director of a religious publishing house who played two important roles in the life of Karl Barth. The first was as editor of the magazine "Between the Times" which, appearing in 1923 acted as the vehicle for the ideas of Barth and the group now gathering around him. ("Mertz is very good", commented Barth on meeting him for the first time, "he knows "Römerbrief" better than I do myself"). The second role was infinitely more important. He introduced Barth to Charlotte Von Kirschbaum, and was to regret doing so for the rest of his life.

Charlotte Emile Henriette Eugenie Von Kirschbaum only daughter of Major General Maximillian Von Kirschbaum and Henrietta, Baroness Von Brück, was born in Ingolstadt, Bavaria on July 25 1899. Her father was killed in action in 1916 on the Western Front while commanding the Sixth Bavarian Infantry Division. In Munich in the early 1920's as a nursing student, then as a Red Cross sister, she moved in those circles in which young people eagerly discussed and lived out the intellectual, artistic, cultural and political developments of the time. It was in such circles that she met George Mertz. By the time she first met Barth it is likely she was already acquainted with his theology.

The decision to launch "Between the Times" had been made at the Bergli, a small summerhouse above Lake Zurich. Barth came to the Bergli every summer vacation, both to relax and to work away from Nelly and the children. Here too came his friends and fellow-activists to stay for a while, to entertain together, to discuss and plan together. Here too came Charlotte Von Kirschbaum with George Mertz in September 1925. The following month, Barth took up his new post as Professor of Dogmatics and New Testament Exegesis at the University of Münster. He lived alone in Münster in rented accommodation until March 1926 when, the Göttingen house finally sold, he was joined by his family. He was therefore still living on his own in Münster when Charlotte Von Kirschbaum came to visit him in February 1926. That summer she spent her vacation with the Barth family. By the summer of 1929 she had moved into the Barth family home where she was to remain for nearly forty years.

She became not only his secretary but also his partner in his work. Barth made no secret that the extent of his work would not have been possible without her. With Nelly Barth relegated into the background his work, which he saw as the most important part of his life, was now carried forward with Charlotte Von Kirschbaum. Each summer was spent together at the Bergli, away from the distraction of his family. Neither of them saw any reason to deny their relationship or to belittle its importance, at least as regards his work. Friends, colleagues and students came to rely on her for help and advice. She was to take a leading part in his controversies, which in time became a dangerous role for a German citizen.

Their friend Gertrude Staewen was to recall in the 1980's: "I can see her before me, living in my memory just as she was in those years when I first knew her. It must have been around 1929. In full bright-blue silk dresses which matched so well her marvellous blue eyes, delicate, with fine features, and sparkling with an energy which was never loud but always present: That energy that courage for living with which she had decided once and for all to be there for only one person, for his work, for his well-being and his happiness, for his friends and students".

A photograph shows the two of them at the Bergli in a summer of the late 1920's. The shutters of an upstairs window are thrown back, the light is streaming in as they sit on either side of a table at the window, a vase of flowers between them. They are both writing, lost in mutual concentration. Gertrude Staewen described how she found the mutual congeniality in which the two of them worked as unforgettable and unrepeatable. "A oneness of intellectual communion". She described, long after they were both dead, how she could still see the great happiness the two of them had in each other and in their work, so evident the evening after Barth finished his book on Anselm; the two of them sitting together in the garden of the Bergli, drinking wine and listening to Mozart amid the scent of the larkspur and phlox.

Rose-Marie Barth, wife of his eldest son Markus, recalls what Eduard Thurneysen said to her when, in 1938/39 she first became acquainted with the Barth household, then living on the Albanring in Basle.

"Eduard Thurneysen... told me that the relationship among the three persons was unique, something that had developed over the years, and I should accept as such without question... At the time I had only a vague idea of what he was talking about, but I soon learned that he was right and his advice was good. The less the gossips in Basle, and especially elsewhere, knew about the house on the Albanring, the more they found to talk about. None of them had any idea how much suffering there was under the roof of that house. But the work of theology was joyful, and the involvement in that work, to whatever extent, held the three together through toils and perils".

There are many, very many, books on Karl Barth. In some mention is made of Charlotte von Kirschbaum as his collaborator. There are no books on Nelly Barth and she receives no credit for his achievements in theology. One observation may be hazarded about Nelly Barth; she surely bore the greatest share of that suffering which took place under Barth's roof.

The title of George Mertz's magazine "Between the Times" came from an earlier article by the young German theologian Friedrich Gogarten, one of those now grouped with Barth and a visitor to the Bergli. Other prominent members of the group were Emil Brunner and Rudolph Bultmann. Beginning as a student of art history and psychology, Gogarten had studied theology under von Harnack. Theology by itself proved unsatisfactory as a means of understanding the riddle posed by our existence and he again widened his studies. Philosophy and Tolstoy and Kierkegaard were all brought within the sphere of his searching mind. For a while he lived in Florence, played the cello and wrote a book on German philosophy. Thurneysen had been the first to be impressed by Gogarten and wrote to Barth: "I am astonished at the extent of common ground between him and us. He comes from a completely different side of us, has wandered along all the detours and by-ways of .... mysticism and romanticism, but now stands near us". When Barth finally met Gogarten he was most impressed: "Here is a dreadnought for us and our opponents. Who knows, perhaps one day yet he will teach us something!"

Gogarten was forthright in expressing what he felt to be the stance of his generation: "It is the destiny of our generation to stand between the times. We never belonged to the period presently coming to an end: it is doubtful whether we shall ever belong to the period which is to come... So we stand in the middle - in an empty space". He rejected utterly the traditional authorities in culture, politics and religion, all that had been inherited from the 19th Century. "Today we are witnessing the demise of your world. We can be as calm about all that concerns this decline as if we were seeing the extinction of something with which we have no connection at all... And now we are glad for the decline, for no-one enjoys living among corpses".

Unsuspected by either Barth or Gogarten the cause of their future breach already lay between them. Not in Gogarten's suggestion that 'Between The Times' be entitled 'The Word' — rather call it 'Ship of Fools' Barth had retorted. Not even that at the beginning of the Great War Gogarten had published a pamphlet urging that the War be grasped as a positive opportunity for the rise of a new spirit throughout Germany. Instead the breach lay hidden in the common language which united them both. There was much mutual talk and writing of 'crisis'; the dramatic and frequent use of 'crisis' had been a much-noted feature of 'Römerbrief' and was much used now by Gogarten. But for Gogarten 'crisis' is the description of the acute malaise of those times, whereas for Barth it is the situation in which humanity is always standing before God.

Gertrude Staewen, the friend of Barth and Charlotte von Kirschbaum was, in some respects, typical of that new generation described by Gogarten. Brought up in Bremen, in the stiff confines of a narrow puritanical Christianity, with a father who could scarcely comprehend that Germany had lost the war and that the Kaiser had abdicated. Though he believed women should not have an education, the social and economic collapse of 1918 enabled her father to be persuaded that she travel to Berlin to train in voluntary social work.

In her early twenties she arrived in a Berlin fermenting with artistic and political ideas, and eagerly attended Social Democrat meetings and marxist debates. She became part of the Youth Movement, a term used to cover the multitude of diverse youth groups, each rebelling against the past in some way, and all in search of a better future. Journeying in whatever time they had free, as if on a pilgrimage. Through the mountains and forests, singing, reading Göethe, seeking to become closer to nature. Those wandering far a-field throughout Europe and beyond were called the Wandervogel. Some of the ideas of the Youth Movement were crystallised in a popular novel "Der Wunderapostel". A wandering Indian seeks a "ripe soul" to inherit the sacred learning of the East which alone can bring rebirth to a stricken Europe. The "ripe soul" is discovered to be a German youth, musical, in communion with nature and who will become the one to bring about the healing of nations.

Though involved in the Youth Movement an astringency and tough-mindedness in Gertrude Staewen prevented her from taking it with a final seriousness. It was this quality which led to her life-long friendship with Karl Barth.

On the left wing of the broad spectrum of the Youth Movement she was at a gathering of religious socialists in Berlin in 1922. Some stood up and explained their theories for social reform; others recited from their poems; others passages from the novels they were writing. All this, she recalled "to promote socialism and improve human beings. A great deal of totally idealistic rubbish that wasn't true, to make us all more Christian and more socialist". Then someone spoke of how the novel could lead a person to Christ. She could keep quiet no longer, and jumped to her feet shouting out that no novel could ever bring anyone to Christ. Then she paused for a moment and added that perhaps she might make an exception in the case of Dostoevsky.

At this a man who until then had been sitting silently at the back of the crowded room rose and came up to her.

"Do you know my friend Eduard Thurneysen?" he asked.

"No".

"Then read him".

This was Barth. She thought he looked like a wood cut of a Swiss farmer. It is unclear whether she ever read Thurneysen's book on Dostoevsky but she did begin to read Barth's "Römerbrief". "I read in it night after night... that was the real turning point in my life".

She was not alone in Germany at that time in being able to say that.

The English writer D H Lawrence had some experience of the Youth Movement and the Wandervogel and they had aroused in him a deep apprehension. In 1924, he contributed "a letter from Germany" to the magazine "New Statesman". He described his journey from Paris through the Marne country, the villages still with their streets of smashed houses, Strasbourg with its shop signs now in French and glutted with cheap cotton goods from factories that once were German. Then across the Rhine into a forsaken land of frozen fields and dark hills. To Baden-Baden, long deserted by its fashionable guests with less and less work and shopkeepers in despair, while through the streets pass wagons taking German timber away to France. Up the Rhine Valley to Heidelberg a university city full of young people with rucksacks and their "non-materialistic professions, their half mystic assertions". They struck Lawrence as somehow primitive, roving gangs from broken and scattered tribes.

Standing in the woods above Heidelberg, he looked out over the ruined castle and peaked roofs of the old city and the glimmer and haze of the river. He now sensed that, for Germany, the years were no longer moving forward but instead were wheeling backwards. "Like a spring that is broken, and whirls swiftly back, so time seems to be whirling with mysterious swiftness to a sort of death. Whirling to the ghost of the Middle Ages of Germany, then to the Roman days, then to the days of the silent Forest and lurking barbarians". On this 1924 journey he became aware of something new. "Out of the very air comes a sense of danger, a queer *bristling* feeling of uncanny danger..... Something has happened. Something has happened which has not yet eventuated.... The last two years have done it. The hope in peace and production is broken.... back, back to the savage polarity of Tartary and away from the polarity of civilised Christian Europe... it is the father of the next phase of events ... at the same time we have brought it about ourselves – by a Ruhr occupation, by an English nullity and by a German false will, we have done it ourselves but apparently it was not to be helped."

On a summer evening a few years later in Florence two German youths strode out of the shadows of a side-street into the full flood of evening sunlight over the banks of the Arno. They were of the "true Wandervogel type" with shorts, boots and rucksacks with open-necked shirts and faces dark tanned by the sun. Lawrence wondered whether they were leaving Florence, pressing on "to get out of the Porta Romano before nightfall going southwards".

Then he wondered why he was wondering about them, about where they were going and why. Wandervogel were often to be seen on the streets of Florence that year. Why then, each time they appeared, did he catch himself wondering about them, about the impression they created in him. "If swans or wild geese flew honking low over the Arno in the evening light, moving with that wedge-shaped, intent, unswerving progress that is so impressive they would create the same impression in one. They would bring that sense of remote, far-off lands which these Germans bring, and that sense of mysterious, unfathomable purpose".

This sense, this intuition, was surely mistaken. He knew perfectly well that Munich and Frankfurt were not in the least in a remote and far-off land, quite the contrary. There was nothing unfathomable surely about modern Germany. He only had to look at the middle-class German tourists around him. "They are *so* bourgeois, so much more a product of civilisation than the producers of civilisation. They are *so* buttoned up inside their waistcoats, are stuck inside their trousers, and encircled in their starched collars. They are not so grotesquely self-conscious and physically withered or non-existent as the equivalent English bourgeois tourist. And they are never quite so utterly domesticated as the equivalent Scandinavian. But they have so often the unsure look of children who have been turned out in their best clothes by their Mama, and told to go and enjoy themselves: "Now enjoy yourselves"."

Neither was there anything mysterious about the younger people from other countries. As for those young "English people with rucksacks and shirt sleeves rolled back and hob-nailed boots", the only notable thing about them was how little impression they made upon him. Whereas whenever Wandervogel appeared they gave him "a strong feeling of *somewhere else*, of an unknown country, an unknown race, a powerful, still unknown north land".

Sitting in the evening sunshine he thought of the astonishment the citizens of Imperial Rome must have felt when they first encountered a Germanic tribesman with his "insolent-indifferent blue eyes standing looking on in the market places". Though they did not know it they were seeing for the first time one of the men who were to overthrow and destroy the Roman Empire and bring in a new world.

This was the direction to which he found his thoughts turning that evening, watching the two Wandervogel striding away like wild geese winging south. "Strange wanderers towards the sun, forerunners of another world of men. That is how one still feels, as one sees Wandervogel cross the Ponte Vecchio. They carry with them another world, another air, another meaning of life."

CHAPTER 7

To many in the Protestant Church the bitterness and despair of wartime defeat had been crowned by the advent of Adolf "Ten Commandments" Hoffman.

The social upheavals, called by some the Revolution, of November 1918 had brought Adolf Hoffman to take charge of state policy towards the church in Prussia. A radical left-wing socialist, an agitator at mass rallies who liked to give his audience the benefit of his wit, member and champion of the Proletariat, he had earned his nickname by a speech exposing the Ten Commandments as a tool of the capitalist ruling class. One photograph shows him in action at a mass rally, a full head of fluffy white hair, white moustaches and an impressive goatee, the large audience no doubt enjoying the benefit of his denunciations and his biting wit. A man of decided character, so decided as to be etched as a familiar type. Now was Hoffman's chance to show the churches a thing or two, those tools of a ruling class now irreversibly consigned by the laws of historical development to the dustbin of history. He issued a number of far-reaching decrees, quite illegal but founded on his revolutionary right and the backing of the bayonets of the Berlin Workers and Soldiers Councils.

One decree abolished all state subsidies to the churches. This wiped out more than half the budget of the Protestant Churches in Prussia. Another decree abolished religious instruction in schools and the Christian character of schools. These decrees succeeded in achieving what many had thought impossible. They brought together - for a brief moment -the Protestant and Catholic Churches who jointly concluded that the differences between them were as nothing to the abyss which separated them both from Adolf Hoffman. Hoffman lasted only six weeks. He walked out of the Government, together with other radical left-wing Socialists; naturally on a point of principle. The practical problems he created were to be resolved in time by a series of compromises between the Government and the Churches. But the venom he injected into Church-State relations was lasting. He convinced a great majority in the Protestant Church - many of whom needed little persuading - that the abolition of Christianity was an item on the Socialist agenda for Germany. The Social Democrats were therefore tainted from the start. Large numbers in the churches could not see in the Weimar

Republic any trace of moral principle, could see no religious justification for its constitution, and in the figure of Adolf Hoffman, the symbol of the worst of all possible threats to the Christian religion.

Barth's years at Göttingen had been filled not only with teaching but also with study. No longer a village pastor he became only too aware of how much he had yet to learn, especially when compared with the deep erudition of Emmanuel Hirsch. For the next few years his publications would be mainly in the form of articles. There were also other demands on his time and energy. "Not only did I have to keep on learning and learning, but as the representative of a new theological trend, I also had to show my credentials and save my skin in every possible circle by giving lectures and holding public discussions". These took him all over Germany and he saw himself as a commercial traveller, with his briefcase, on platforms and in waiting rooms, jumping from express trains and hurrying to catch the connecting local service. Speaking in cities and towns, at times addressing audiences of more than 1,000, travelling north and south, east and west, meeting scholars and pastors, students and lay-people, beginning to appreciate for the first time the great size and diversity of Germany.

"Then suddenly to the station at a gallop and, after many hours on the express, somewhere there appears the familiar image of a conference: grey ministerial figures, excited young ones, blond-bearded liberals with glasses... at Lüneburg: an old-fashioned little town, houses with thick stone gables such as one might see in a dream... Elgersburg: a sea of greeny autumn, Thuringian woods, green, red, yellow and one among many farm villages in it with white gables and timber frames, and in the middle of that, an old castle... Bochum: countless factory chimneys and fantastic machines, the air full of coal dust... the East Friesians and the Benteimers... the black coats came from all sides through the endless avenues of trees, past windmills and dykes... the North German Lowland has made a great impression upon me: it has a striking quality, the windmills like Apocalyptic question marks, full of movement... Danzig is delightful, a real fairy tale of Hanseatic splendour, brick Gothic, bold Baroque, and ornamented Rococo. The Hanseatic cities are some of the best things in Germany... the Saint Mary's Church here with the Memling "Last Judgement" is a fine thing. Of course, one always feels some anxiety (already in Lübeck I felt it) about the connection of the *old* middle class society to the church. These private pews (i.e.: whole little houses built inside the church, each in part with its own heating!) of the patricians tell the tale only too naively of how those robust old pepper sacks and sea robbers thought of the matter and then all the epitaphs and the pictures of the old preachers and their ruffled collars and with the Bible under their arm who sanctioned all those things from the pulpits which, to some extent, looked like citadels and the angels with trumpets who for three hundred years now have been puffing out their golden cheeks. Think of all that the dear God has had to experience with the people! This evening, then, an encounter with all the men who now stand in these pulpits".

Contrary to the expectations of those such as Adolf Hoffman, the Church did not wither away during the years of the Weimar Republic. No longer tied to the ruling houses of the Kaiser's Reich, the Church was now free to reform its structure. There was founded in 1922 at Wittenberg - with appropriate ceremony and solemnity - the German Evangelical Federation of Churches which enabled action to be taken as necessary at national level. Real power however, lay with the twenty-eight provincial churches, the Landeskirchen, which composed the Federation. Of the twenty-eight Landeskirchen of the Evangelical Federation, fifteen were Lutheran and one Reformed, with twelve Union where Lutheran and Reformed Churches were united for administrative purposes. Largest and most important by far was the Union Church of the Old Prussian Union. With freedom to govern their own affairs some of the Landeskirchen chose Bishops to head their governing bodies, other chose Presidents, while the Old Prussian Union had a system of General Superintendents.

Much remained untouched by these reforms. In the minds of most of the clergy and church members the unity of throne and altar had been simply replaced by the union of altar and nation and the nation was definitely not to be identified with the Weimar Republic. The old ruling and political order had been swept away, the government of the church had been reformed, but religion was still wedded with nationalism, a marriage bond made even stronger by Germany's sufferings.

As the economy started to improve so did the fortunes of the church and a strong note of optimism and confidence for the future was clearly sounded in the book "The Century of the Church" by Otto Dibelius, youngest General Superintendent of the Old Prussian Union. During the War, in this most nationalistic of churches, he had not been afraid to urge that the Church should "give Christian pacifists its blessing, even when it does not approve of their stand.". Now, in the "Century of the Church" he saw the true meaning of November 1918 as a "liberating storm" which had freed the Church for its new task. This task being to defend Christian values and moral standards in an intellectual and political culture which no longer acknowledges the validity of such values and standards. A culture which did not realise that life in any community is intolerable, in fact impossible, without values and standards. "Truly", said Dibelius, "it is high time that someone seized the helm with a strong hand, applied the criteria of an absolute morality to the new conditions and restored humanity to an awareness of what is good and what is evil". It was the task of the Church to instil this moral judgement into society. There is no field of social activity which is neutral to the application of moral judgement. It was time for the Church to start asking itself and society such questions as: "is there a limit to the profit which the producer gets from his goods? What is the relationship between the right of capital and the right of the worker? How do things stand with the claim of the State on the life of its citizens?" As it proposed a vital task, a crucial role, for the Church in the new conditions of society Dibelius' "The Century of the Church" proved to be both popular and influential. Karl Barth thought it was "without exaggeration a worthless book".

Weimar may now be the capital of Germany but Berlin has become the capital of a new kind of country, one without boundaries or frontiers.

Experimental art and design flourishes and new forms of drama are born. Huge film studios are opened and audiences flock to see films the like of which have never been made elsewhere: in a city of the future a beautiful robot is created to betray the workers; a city's murderers and thieves band together to track down a serial child-killer; a madman manipulates a somnambulist and a master-criminal uses hypnosis to dominate a society descending into chaos.

Cabarets and reviews flourish in such profusion as nowhere else, dispensing liquor and life-enhancing nihilism. A guide to the city describes the favoured area for lesbians, male homosexuals and transvestites. This is a city to be recalled later by one Berliner: "Within the city millions of underfed, corrupt, sex-starved and pleasure hungry men and women writhe and totter in a jazz induced delirium. Dance has become a mania, an obsession, a cult. The Stock Exchange hops like a frog, ministers sway on their feet, the Reichstag does a jig, war cripples and profiteers, film stars and prostitutes, former monarchs (with princely pensions) and retired school masters (with no pensions at all) — all twist and turn in gruesome euphoria."

The progress of the Evangelical Federation itself appeared to justify Dibelius optimism. For example, by the end of the decade more than six hundred independent church papers had been founded with a total circulation of about 70 million and the number of theological students had tripled to five and a half thousand.

For many in the church this was evidence that the church had won through, the Gates of Hell had not prevailed against it. The arguments, hostility and mockery of the atheists, agnostics and sceptics had proved futile. The Godless Weimar culture, worshipping only what was modern, licentious and decadent had not succeeded in drowning morality under its flood. While there were still worrying rates of defection, particularly among the urban working-class, the bedrock of support in the middle-classes had not been washed away. There was now much talk of how masterly the church leadership had been to steer the church through the time of testing and crises. A time, thankfully, now past. During the early Weimar years intellectuals and assorted communists had assailed Christianity with all the arguments at their disposal. Their complete failure in the face of the staunchness of the church was now there for all the world to see. While whatever destination the Youth Movement and the Wandervogel were striding or aiming towards was certainly not membership of the German Evangelical Federation, the bourgoise at least now felt comfortable in their own church.

Even at Safenwil, Barth had been suspicious of all talk of church or Christian successes. What, he asked "In the ministry, is satisfaction? Do the Prophets and Apostles, not to speak of Jesus Christ, give us the impression of people who have succeeded, who could at the end look back upon a blessed and satisfying life? Strange that we do so much better than they! ... Upon what grounds do you assume the role of mediator between Heaven and Earth? Who has authorised you to take your place there and generate religious feeling and, to crown all, to do so with results, with success? Did one ever hear of such overwhelming presumption ..."

Barth now had two specific reasons to feel increasingly disturbed with the church in Germany. First, the leading groups and organs of opinion within the church were strongly biased in favour of the forces of political reaction. On this he considered that, as a Swiss, he had best refrain from public statements. The second was "now that for the first time it had found its own feet in independence from the state, it developed a remarkably pompous self-importance which did not seem to be matched by the content and profundity of its preaching. Here and there could be found "Bishops" of the kind who loved being Bishops, and others who very much wanted to be Bishops. And some of them, pooh-poohing the malice of the time and the storm clouds in the heavens, saw the star of the whole "Century of the Church" rising on the horizon. I could not see either of these tendencies as being of any use to the course of the church and opposed them as well as I could".

His first attack came in a public lecture towards the end of 1929. "Would it not be appropriate... to proceed with greater caution in using the adjective "Christian" than has become customary in victorious modern Christendom? What is meant by Christian world-view, Christian morality, Christian art? What are Christian personalities, Christian families, Christian circles, Christian parties, and Christian newspapers... Who gives us permission to use this predicate so lavishly, especially when we have to know that the conferring of this adjective in its proper, serious sense, is completely withdrawn from our authority?"

He followed this with an article in which he ridiculed all talk of crises being mastered, of masterpieces of church leadership and described all such talk as that of a church which, shameless in its lack of restraint, desires and praises only itself.

Such attacks could not go unanswered and Dibelius in particular responded to Barth in a series of articles and speeches. He criticised Barth as a theoretician, unable to grasp the actual practice and needs of the church and the challenges of the real world which the church faced. Barth did not realise that in pursuing its mission in the Godless Weimar Republic the church had been, as Dibelius explained, "forced into a battle more serious than any conducted since the cross of Christ was first carried upon German soil".

Even then that soil was preparing a new growth. One of the seeds from which grew the Faith Movement of German Christians was planted in Thuringia by two neighbouring pastors, Siegfried Leffler and Julius Leutheuser. Both twenty-eight years old at that time they were both unusual in that they were members of the National Socialist German Workers Party - The NSDAP or Nazi Party. Unusual in that even as late as 1931 the likely number of pastors who were members of the Nazi Party was around 100 out of an Evangelical Federation total of approximately 18,000.

In the years following the Great War they had studied theology in Bavaria. Study and daily experience convinced them that the church had failed and that theology was out of touch with real life. Dead orthodoxy was more important to the theologians than the needs of the People. A self-important leadership and bureaucracy, perpetuating itself through the propagation of stale doctrines and regulations, was incapable of love for the people. Only in the Nazi Party did they find the necessary love of the People, and the challenge to sacrifice their lives in the service of that love, so utterly lacking in the church. In their neighbouring pastorates they began using the Youth Movement, of which they had been members, as a model for community activism. There were youth evenings, literature study groups, theatre groups. No distinction was made between church, cultural and political activity. All was a unity of faith and action, devoid of the church "tendency to turn away from the world, nature and life".

They were led on their progress "with a heart full of awe and faith" by the example of the leader of the Nazi Party who was active in self-giving for and to the German People. Leffler was later to explain "the fact of the matter is that in the pitch-dark night of Christian church history Hitler became, as it were, the wonderful transparency, the window of our age, through which light fell on the history of Christianity. Through him we were able to see the Saviour in the history of the Germans".

As Dibelius and Barth quarrelled the event whose consequences were to destroy the German Evangelical Federation had already occurred half a world away. In October 1929 the New York Stock Exchange collapsed and its fall blew away the German economic recovery. Millions were thrown out of work, savings wiped out, pensions disappeared, the country gripped again by poverty and fear. Emmanuel Hirsch wrote to a Danish friend "You do not know how great the despair is among us simply because we have no food and no work for one quarter of the People and this winter it will become one third of the People". Gold and bankers and the markets had done Germany down and the old politics had failed. It was time to heed new voices.

In September 1930 the elections for the Reichstag were held. With 6½ million votes cast in its favour, with its parliamentary seats increased from 12 to 107, the National Socialist German Workers Party leapt from the margins to become the second strongest political party in Germany.

CHAPTER 8

Emmanuel Hirsch was one of the many who believed the Weimar Republic to be the grave of a great nation and who longed for a resurrection. There were those who believed the dead could be raised.

From the very beginning Hitler's voice was full of confidence. Addressing shabby crowds in smoke-filled beer-cellars and dance halls, in cobbled squares and in the streets where the poor gathered. The confidence of one who knew that he was acting in accordance with the will of his Almighty Creator. There were many in Germany who had little time for him or the sort of people who were his followers, and they called him a rabble-rouser. If so, he was not the first, as he told the crowd in a Munich beer-cellar in April 1922, "My Christian feeling points me towards my Lord and Saviour as a fighter. It points me towards the man who, once lonely and surrounded by only a few followers, ... who, as true God, was not only the greatest as a sufferer but also the greatest as a warrior. In boundless love, as a Christian and a human being, I read the passage which declares to us how the Lord finally rose up and seized a whip to drive the Usurers, the brood of serpents and vipers from the Temple!"

As the cellar began to fill with applause his voice grew ever louder to rise above it. "Today, however, two thousand years later, I am deeply moved to perceive that his tremendous struggle for this world against the Jewish poison was most profoundly marked by the fact that he had to bleed on the cross for it". He now had to shout over the clamour in the hall. "Two thousand years ago a man was also denounced by this race... the man was dragged before the court and it was also said of him "he stirred up the people". So he too had been a "rabble-rouser" and against whom? Against God they cried. Yes, indeed he roused the rabble against the God of the Jews for this God is only gold". This climax was greeted with tumultuous applause and he was so pleased by this speech that he had it printed and distributed.

A few years earlier, at the age of thirty, Adolf Hitler sketched out the conclusions of his own study of the Bible. It had to be purged of all that was Jewish. To the very end, he maintained, what was needed was a return to the original and true teachings of Jesus. Even as late as 1944 he informed Martin Bormann that Jesus had fought "against the depraved materialism of his time and thus against the Jews". He also told Bormann that it was Paul who had first, in a subtle way, falsified the teachings of Christ.

Such ideas were common currency in certain German intellectual circles. For many years there had been calls for a return to the true religion of Jesus. Christianity as was now proclaimed and practised, in both Catholic and Protestant churches, was a distortion of the true and original Gospel. The root of the distortion being Paul who, in the words of one writer, "had brought the Old Testament into the church, and through his influence the Gospel has been ruined, as far as this is possible". For another, Paul is "the poisoner of the religious source and the false teacher... this arch-enemy of Jesus". Against the perversions of Paul and the materialism of the Jews the German people had to rediscover their natural spirituality. As the Munich author Dietrich Eckart explained "to be an Aryan and to sense transcendence is one and the same thing". Eckart's phrase "Germany Awake" became the battle cry of the Nazi Party.

While having his intellectual roots in such circles, Adolf Hitler concluded that his path to power could only be achieved through the creation and organisation of a mass political party, not by a religious movement. To gain power, to become Führer of the German people, he needed the support of the ordinary Christians, of Prussian protestants and the catholics of Bavaria. This would not be achieved if the Nazi Party were identified as opposed to the established churches, if it became mired and distracted in inevitably divisive debates about religious ideas. The title of the Nazi Party, the "National Socialist German Workers Party" was chosen for that very reason. Such a title, he explained, "kept away the antiquity enthusiasts".

Nothing could be clearer than the point made in his first public statement following his release from imprisonment after his failed coup. The February 1925 Article "On the Resurrection of our Movement" reviewed the current situation and assured his followers that the struggle continued. A struggle not to be diverted by religious controversy. "At this point I must object especially to the attempt to try to drag religious disputes into the Movement, indeed to equate the Movement with them". That he was perfectly serious in this, and the reasons why, are evident from the case of Doctor Dinter.

Doctor Artur Dinter had been a science teacher in Strassburg, then an author, a dramatist and a theatre director in Rostock and Berlin. He was a member of the inner most circle of the Party with Party membership N05, and leader of the Party in Thuringia. At the height of their disagreement Hitler could still describe him as "Dear Herr Doctor whom I personally admire". Dinter's ambition was the creation of a German church which would unite all German Christians in a return to the pure teachings of Jesus. A purely Aryan Christianity, with the Jewish Old Testaments and Jewish-Christian dogma eliminated. Summed up in Dinter's slogan "Down with the Old Testament! Down with Paul! Back to Christ!"

A study of history convinced Dinter that religious revolutions, the heightening of spiritual and moral consciousness, always proceed epoch-making political revolutions - never the other way around. National Socialism would fail if it remained a merely political struggle. "It will only conquer and can only conquer when it lays the axe to the spiritual roots of Judaism, that is, to Judaism in the Christian church".

Contrary to Hitler's pronouncement that the National Socialist Movement must not be equated with religious disputes, Dinter campaigned loudly for supremacy of the spiritual revolution over the political. His efforts attracted sufficient publicity for a senior committee of the Party to look into his activities, and then pass a resolution urging Dinter to stop his religious propagandising; if not he would face expulsion from the Party. Hitler himself sent the resolution to Dinter under cover of a long letter in which, in respectful tones, he explained that the Party Committee was quite correct in perceiving the absolute priority of political action. "The fate of our People, at least to the extent that it is a race problem, will be decided in less time than the carrying out of a religious reformation was called for. Either our People will tear itself away as quickly as possible from the ruin that faces it, especially racially, or it will perish in the process". Then, remarkably, he forecasts that he probably has only twenty years still available to him. Sufficient for the victory of a political movement "if fate does not decide otherwise" but much too short to effect a religious reformation. Hitler ends the letter: "Should you feel the need, Dear Doctor, to speak to me personally, I would welcome it very much and would be at your disposal at any time". Two months later, at the beginning of September 1928, Hitler took the opportunity of a major Party Conference to repeat his determination that the Movement be kept free of all religious disputes. Dinter's reply was an article attacking Hitler for his blindness to the Jewish elements in Christianity. Doctor Artur

Dinter had little reason to be surprised when he was expelled from the Party the following month.

In order to make clear that the Party was not opposed to any of the Christian denominations a demand for religious freedom - except for Jews - was included in the Party programme along with other Nazi social demands.

We demand abolition of incomes unearned by either work or effort.

We demand nationalisation of all trusts.

We demand profit sharing in large concerns.

We demand the extensive development of Old Age Pensions.

We demand land reform adapted to our national needs.

We demand the education of intellectually gifted children of poor parents without regard to class or occupation, and at the expense of the State.

The State must take care of improvements in Public Health through protection of mothers and children, through prohibiting child labour...

We demand liberty for all religious confessions in the State, insofar as they do not in any way endanger its existence or do not offend the moral sentiments and the customs of the Germanic race. The Party as such represents the standpoint of "positive Christianity" without binding itself confessionally to a particular faith. It opposes the Jewish materialist spirit within and without and is convinced that permanent recovery of our people is possible only from within and on the basis of the general principle of: General Welfare Before Individual Welfare.

That Christ was a Jew has always been a source of disquiet to Christianity and Emmanuel Hirsch was among those who have attempted the removal of this embarrassment. During the Third Reich Emmanuel Hirsch published a book containing a number of lectures on the essence of Christianity. Comparison of the two Testaments confirmed that Jesus inaugurated an entirely new and unique religion. The Old Testament is about the Jewish People: Contrary to this Jesus creates a universal religion. Jesus' racial origins were also examined by Hirsch. Careful textual analysis of the Gospels with their ambiguities when contrasted with each other concerning Jesus birth and family tree, together with the results of historical research into the patterns of ethnic settlements in Galilee, yield the same conclusions.

"According to all the rules of scientific probability, Jesus was of non-Jewish blood".

In the game of historical appropriation and reinterpretation there is hardly a more popular piece than Jesus Christ. Even in the time of Schleiermacher there were already a number of Jesus Christs in circulation among the theologians, the results of eighteenth century historical study of the Gospels. There was the Jesus preaching simple truths misunderstood by the superstitious of the time and there was also the Jesus who used the superstitions of the time as a means to worldly power. Among the more notable additions of the nineteenth century is the Jesus of David Strauss, inseparable and indistinguishable from the adoring myths woven by the earliest Christians. During the remainder of that century there appeared several varieties of Jesus who survived the crucifixion, as well as Jesus the Essene, Jesus the Aryan and Jesus the Buddhist as proven by documents hidden in a monastery in Tibet. In a crowded field the most successful was the Jesus discovered by Ernst Renan. A charismatic young carpenter and teacher who with infinite tenderness spoke eloquently of the Kingdom of Heaven. Wandering through an idyllic landscape in the company of his idealistic young followers and winning hearts, specially of women, with his charm and his discourse of divine love, participating reluctantly in false miracles only so as not to disappoint the expectations of the more simple. With such a pedigree the appearance of Jesus as an anti-Jewish Socialist was inevitable.

Hirsch's own politics and theology developed with logic and passion. They could not in any event be divided from each other. Neither were abstractions to be divorced from each other or from life. God, as he had explained to Barth, can be encountered only in the accusations and demands of the conscience.

Years earlier he had set out his hopes for how Germany could be saved by Christianity. "We Germans must become a pious People, a People in which the Gospel has power over conscience. Otherwise we will not be masters of our fate... Belief in God awakens exactly the qualities of character and soul which we Germans now require so very much... Belief in God creates men, men of unshakable desire for freedom and genuine faithfulness, whose will no person can break in two and men with warm hearts, who are capable of a complete and strong love for their People, even when they gain nothing personally from this love, even when this People behaves ever so wildly and foolishly".

Written in 1920 this could perhaps be seen as a prefigurement of how Adolf Hitler came to see and present himself.

Hitler confessed in `Mein Kampf': "Hence today I believe that I am acting in accordance with the will of the Almighty Creator: by defending myself against the Jews, I am fighting for the work of the Lord". In the 1928 Reichstag elections the National Socialist German Workers Party gained only 2.6% of the vote. An insignificant party, it was going nowhere. A few months later, only days after he had expelled Doctor Artur Dinter from the Party, Hitler took the opportunity during a speech in Passau to spell out what he saw as the consequences of that expulsion.

"This movement has gained a remarkable freedom of operation which in the supreme sense of the word allows the rejection of anything which could in any way divide the People. We are a People of different faiths but we are one. We tolerate no one in our ranks who offends against the ideas of Christianity, who offers resistance to someone with another disposition, fights against him or acts as archenemy of Christianity. This, our Movement, is in fact Christian. We are filled with a desire for Catholics and Protestants to discover one another in the deep distress of our People. We shall suppress any attempt to put religious issues on the Agenda of our Movement".

As in the beginning his voice is full of confidence.

CHAPTER 9

The Nazis were once young. Once they were the young. In the storm of ruin and misery brought by the Great Depression it was the young who seized the offer of radical protest and renewal. In the years leading up to the Third Reich the Nazis had by far the youngest membership of any major political party. In December 1930 a church newspaper reported a theological student as explaining that almost all the students of theology at his university were Nazis. The following month, a pastor in Berlin informed the church authorities that not only was the influence of national socialism on Protestant youth extremely strong, it was also, in his opinion to be welcomed from a religious point of view. Explaining that all his best former and present confirmation candidates were Nazis "the self-discipline of the young Nazis is nothing short of exemplary and automatically raises them above the others, involuntarily giving them a position of leadership. From the Church's point of view, therefore, I welcome this Movement."

University teachers did not lag behind their students in open allegiance to radical politics. A December 1930 report in the church newspaper 'Christliche Welt' on the North German Universities stated that about 90% of the Protestant Theologians there were appearing at lectures wearing Nazi Party badges.

The 73 year old editor of the most important of the leading Protestant church papers was not alone in looking upon national socialism as the rebellion of the German youth that "feels deeply the humiliation of the Fatherland, hates and abhors the poisoning of German thought by foreign influences and has ascribed upon its banner the old virtues of truthfulness, honour and loyalty".

There were those who could see no way in which a church which preached brotherly love could compromise with a political party which stirred up racial strife and began its rallies with the cry of "To Hell with the Jews". There were those who considered that the cross and swastika did not necessarily stand in opposition to each other and that the two could be combined in harmony. There were the conservatives, of whom there were many, who looked upon National Socialism simply as a manifestation, if expressed with typical youthful enthusiasm, of a patriotism similar to their own. There were the liberals who opposed, on moral grounds, nationalism of any kind and there were the religious socialists who opposed National Socialism on left wing and ideological grounds. To a large extent however the terms of the growing debate had already been determined by the demands of Hirsch and others that the church's stance be evaluated by the extent to which it supported the German People in the fulfilment of their destiny.

With growing apprehension Barth began to see rising and spreading around him what he was to later call one of the most curious and tragic events in the whole history of Protestant theology. This being the: "Elevation on a wide front, if with varying emphasis, of the term "People" to the front rank of theological and ethical concepts". Despite all the criticism he had made of his theological teachers and forerunners, there was one issue on which Barth would never find them guilty. They would never have given any kind of personal or theological support to the national socialists. Whilst Schleiermacher was one of the great German patriots in the War of Liberation against Napoleon, it was inconceivable that he would have given support of any kind to Hitler. As for the aristocratic von Harnack, Barth thought that he would sooner have become a capuchin monk than be associated with those who were now emerging as the champions of the People.

The Dehn Case helped clarify the coming battle lines. The origins were in 1928 when the theologian Günter Dehn, gave a lecture in Magdeburg on the church and reconciliation between nations. In the course of this lecture Dehn condemned every glorification of war while at the same time dismissing pacifism as naive. War should only be contemplated as the last act of self-defence, while Christians should avoid giving war a Christian face. The custom of the church in identifying death for ones country with pure sacrificial death was rejected; such an identification ignores the fact that the one who was killed had himself also been prepared to kill. The audience was invited to consider for themselves whether it was right to erect war memorials in churches and to have such an institution as the military chaplaincy.

In the outrage which followed he was accused of insulting Germany's fallen heroes, comparing them to murderers. When in December 1930 Dehn accepted an invitation to take up a post at the University of Heidelburg, a newspaper reminded its readers of the Magdeburg lecture. As the Heidelburg students were already rioting against the presence of a Jewish Professor, the university authorities thought it prudent to back away from appointing Dehn. He therefore accepted an alternative offer from the University of

Halle. When Dehn tried to give his first lecture at Halle the whole of the entrance hall of the building and the square in front of it was filled with students shouting "Dehn Out". The general opinion was that the students were simply showing an excess of youthful idealism. Dehn's reply was to publish his own account of this matter. He concluded by drawing attention to what he thought was its real significance. "It could be that the church of today stands on the threshold of a most difficult struggle with modern nationalism, in which our very existence will be endangered. Should I give a gloomy indication of this coming conflict by cowardly yielding and withdrawing from the attack in the interest of my personal equanimity? Here resistance must be given. One cultivates the youth in their current struggles mostly by conceding to and praising their idealism, even if it is leading in the wrong direction. I must express serious reservations about that. Distorted idealism is demonic. It is simply not true that this fanatical love of Fatherland, which in my view is coloured by religion but actually dissociated from God, really helps the Fatherland. On the contrary, it will lead the Fatherland into destruction".

Public positions were now taken up for and against Dehn. In January 1932 Emmanuel Hirsch published an article supporting the students and setting out what should be the minimum qualification for anyone teaching German youth: "The recognition that the nation and its freedom, despite all the questionableness of human existence, remains for the Christian a good thing, hallowed by God. It demands a complete devotion of the heart and the life. And from this recognition follows an endorsement of the passionate will to freedom of our People which is being enslaved and violated by enemies hungry for power and possession".

Barth now felt that he had to add his voice to the debate. The following month he denounced the thinking in political slogans which characterised attacks on Dehn as "a rime of barbarism". Turning explicitly to "Colleague Hirsch" he added "I feel that he and I will never understand each other, either theologically or politically. However, I hope that his and my primary interest lies in theology and not in politics". This was too much for Hirsch. As a Swiss, Barth could not understand the issues involved and yet here he was, pronouncing judgement. Hirsch's passionate love for his country cried out in the open letter he now sent to Barth. "Whoever is not in the position with us to bring tremblingly before God the fate of Germany and to stake his own and his children's existence on that fate, whoever is not called through his very existence to stand with us in our inner self-determination that person also cannot stand in judgement on whether our will is bound on God or not". From the time they had first met ten years before at Göttingen, Barth and Hirsch had repeatedly clashed yet come together again only to clash further; two combatants joined together in mutual opposition. This was a pattern however which required a certain degree of mutual respect. This had now gone. The Dehn Case divided them finally. Though they were to remain locked together in opposition they were never to speak or write directly to each other again.

Many things divided Hirsch and Barth, not least their mutual tendency towards autocracy. Fundamental in the Dehn case and in the conflicts to come were their antithetical views on the relation between theology and politics. At Safenwil Barth had been a passionate socialist but even by the time of the first edition of Römerbrief he had become aware that political principles, no matter how attractive or correct, can lead to a dangerous confusion of the human and divine. One passage in that book has Paul address Barth himself:-

"It goes without saying that you as Christians have nothing to do with monarchies, capitalism, militarism, patriotism and political liberalism... Much closer to *you* of course, is the other possibility of arbitrarily seizing in advance the coming revolution through Christ and thereby impeding it. And I warn *against* this! The matter of divine renewal can, under no circumstance, be confused with human progress. *The divine may not be politicized and that which is human may not be divinized,* not even in favour of democracy and social democracy."

To read Paul's Epistle to the Romans and then to look at the world around is to realise that one is confronted "with the heathen, publicans, Spartacists, imperialists, capitalists and other unsympathetic types – whom God has justified". All political principles are thereby relativised. Theology and church however are inescapably political; even their silence on a particular issue is in principle a political decision to support the status quo. Hirsch acted on the basis of seeking theological justifications for his political beliefs. It was not yet clear how Barth's theology could give support to any political action.

The actual political situation in Germany was now for Barth "like sitting in a car driven by an incompetent or a drunk." So he joined the German Social Democratic Party, not on ideological grounds but as a practical step to identify with the party with the greatest desire for the common decencies of democracy. As for the fascism of the National Socialists this was nothing other than a religion which, in an article of 1931, he described as posing a particular danger to Christians – the danger of temptation.

He explained, as regards Christianity and other religions, that "we are all poor, that we have not found God and never will, that we can never do more than wait for God to find us. Knowing this poverty, Christians know their solidarity with communists, fascists, and the adherents of all other religions. They share the same need and realise that in it there is only one hope. They share the same questions ... Those who believe in God's revelation and know that they must listen and God must speak, are automatically bound up, as it were, with all others.... If the church listens to God's Word, it is the church and not a society engaging in propaganda. ... It need not keep silent, for it may not. It may give offence, for it must. It need not worry about itself. What it has to say to people on the right hand and on the left, whether they like it or not, is gospel, not law. It will preach forgiveness and no obedience but that which springs from forgiveness. It will not oppose a Christian system to religious systems.... Speaking with authority, it will proclaim freedom: freedom of conscience and freedom for others,... It will proclaim this freedom not as an ideal but as a Christmas gift: You *may* be redeemed from bondage to demons because you *are* already redeemed."

The Weimar Republic was dying, denounced by the Left as "social fascism" and by the Right as "traitorism". The impossibility of the present having any kind of a future, of a tension awaiting some apocalyptic outcome was caught by the English poet Stephen Spender then living in Berlin. "In this Berlin, the poverty, the agitation, the propaganda, witnessed by us in the streets and cafes, seemed more and more to represent the whole life of the town, as though there were almost no privacy behind doors. Berlin was a tension, the poverty, the anger, the prostitution, the hope and despair thrown out on to the streets. It was the blatant rich at the smart restaurants, the prostitutes in Army top boots at corners, the grim submerged-looking Communists in processions, and the violent youths who suddenly emerged from nowhere into the Wittenbergplatz and shouted "Germany Awake." "

While growing in numbers, Nazi pastors still made up a very small proportion of the church and were impatient for National Socialism to make the same progress in the church as it was making in the nation. All over Germany small groups of Nazi pastors, such as Leffler and Leutheuser in Thuringia, were attempting to organise so as to work together to greater effect. Early in 1932 a conference of Nazi pastors was held in a tavern in Berlin. Two senior officials of the Party also attended. Agreement was reached on the creation of a new and distinct church party within the German Evangelical Federation. This church party would be quite separate from the Nazi Party, having its own leadership, hierarchy and organisation, and propaganda machinery. It would however have a set of guiding principles which would make it the preferred choice of both Party members and non-members sympathetic to National Socialism. The pastors wished this new church party to be called "Evangelical National Socialists" but the Party officials pointed out that this title was unacceptable. It would introduce the spectre of religious factionalism which Hitler wished to avoid. The title finally agreed was "Faith Movement of German Christians" with Joachim Hossenfelder as national leader.

"A daring band, and perhaps a lost one too". So Joachim Hossenfelder described the circle of predominately very young pastors who came to form the leadership of the German Christians. "They came without exception from the Youth Movement, had almost all been front-line soldiers, wandering between two worlds. In their knapsacks they carried the Greek New Testament, Faust and perhaps even Horace". For them Christianity was not theory or dogma but practice, the fight for social justice. Hossenfelder's deputy, a wartime fighter-pilot now a pastor doing social work among the deprived in Berlin saw his vocation as "to show these hate-filled and disinherited people a concern for justice, for humanity, in this life as well...". The call to put Christianity into practical effect is a strong one, and it was the pastors from the working-class districts who responded most readily to join the German Christians.

Hossenfelder issued a set of guiding principles for the German Christian Movement. Some were in general terms: a vital church must express all the spiritual forces of the People; a stand must be taken on the ground of positive Christianity; there must be profession of an affirmative faith in Christ.

Others were more specific. A fight must be waged against Marxism. Race, the People and nation are orders of existence granted and entrusted to us by God. Faith in Christ deepens and sanctifies ones race.

Two specific proposals revealed the true scope of Hossenfelder's ambitions. One concerned the impersonal bureaucratic structure of an organisation. The other the nature of a particular relationship between men and women. Though seemingly remote there was an essential internal connection. Only if the first proposal was implemented could the second be put into practice. The first proposal was that the twenty-eight Landeskirchen which made up the Evangelical Federation be abolished and replaced by a single Evangelical State Church. The second proposal is that marriage between a German and a Jew be forbidden.

As for the theologians who formed the 'Between The Times' group they had all been growing aware for some time that, as their individual theologies developed, they were beginning to differ from each other in detail. One common factor was emerging however. All the others were beginning to conclude that Barth's theology, by concentrating upon God's revelation in Jesus Christ, completely ignored the reality of the humanity to whom God spoke. His theology was in danger of simply hanging in the air, a timeless dream, unable to speak to the world outside in a language which could be understood.

Rudolph Bultmann thought Barth's main weakness was his ignoring of current philosophy and Barth should begin to think in terms of current existential philosophy.

Emil Brunner pointed out that we must have some natural knowledge of God. "The Gospel does not turn to a person who knows nothing at all".

As for Friedrich Gogarten, Barth's fundamental approach divorced God from history and human life. One cannot write a theology which takes no account of the times in which it is written. Since we live in our own histories, theology cannot be pursued in independence of our historical actuality, our state of life. Also, by virtue of God entering his creation and assuming human nature we have all been given the possibility of meeting Jesus Christ in our own neighbour.

In August 1932 Barth wrote on the present church position. He did not criticise his friends, but he did have some direct criticism of the present state of the Church, including "the constantly increasing confusion, tedium and irrelevance of modern Protestantism which... has lost an entire third dimension – the dimension of what for once, though not confusing it with religious and moral earnestness, we may describe as mystery – with the result that it has been punished with all kinds of worthless substitutes, that it has fallen the more readily victim to such uneasy cliques and sects as High Church, German Church, Christian Community and Religious Socialism, and that many of its preachers and adherents have finally learned to discover deep religious significance in the intoxication of Nordic blood and their political Führer".

He was still not prepared to attack publicly Gogarten and other colleagues but his doubts and fears were expressed in a letter to Thurneysen. "My dear Eduard, a very bad business is brewing all along the line which I want under no circumstances to have any part of. Is it not true that gradually all of the people who apparently stood close to us want something which we … did not want and which stands in the closest possible connection with, if it is not identical to, that which we fought against from the very beginning… "

Faced with the increasing number of political murders the Weimar Government issued in August 1932 an emergency decree providing for the death penalty in such cases. That very night five SA men, the Nazi Brownshirts, in the small village of Potempa forced their way into the home of a Communist worker, dragged him from his bed, and kicked him to death in front of his mother. These five men from Potempa were the first to be arrested, tried, and sentenced to death under the new decree.

Hitler could not contain his outrage, sending the condemned men a telegram. "In view of this most monstrous blood-judgement, I feel committed to you with unbounded loyalty. From this moment on your freedom is a question of our honour. It is our duty to fight a Government under which this is possible!" From his cell one of the condemned let it be known that this telegram had joined Hitler's photograph on the wall of his cell as the small altar before which he prayed daily.

Following street-fighting in the city of Altona between Nazis and Communists which left 17 dead and over 100 injured, the pastors there prepared a statement on the relationship between Christianity and politics. Among other matters the statement claimed that while we are required to be obedient to political power each of us must decide, if the moment comes, whether to obey God rather than men. This work by the Altona pastors was attacked by both the Communists and the Nazis. In the Communist response can be heard a last echo of Adolf Hoffmann. "The perpetuation of the misery of the masses, oppression and war... A more than heavy-handed attempt at deception by the church... Now more than ever mass resignation!" The Nazis were more succinct. Pointing out that the Altona pastors obviously did not understand the times they were living in, a Party newspaper helpfully explained, "anyone who is not for us is against us - or as far as we are concerned, he is dead". This was January 1933 and by the end of the month Adolf Hitler was Chancellor of Germany.

CHAPTER 10

Hermann Göering announced to the great crowd waiting in the Wilhelmstrasse "Adolf Hitler has become Reich Chancellor".

When evening fell the triumph began. From out of the darkness of Berlin came column after column of marching men, singing as they marched. Tens of thousands upon tens of thousands. In their brown shirts and high boots, marching in disciplined ranks to the rhythmic beating of the drums. Each man carrying a flaming torch, the marching columns merging into a single river of light and song. As the flowing river filled up the heart of the capital the vast crowds of spectators broke into prolonged shouts of enthusiasm, all caught up into one rhythm, one voice, one exultation.

Powerful columns of men were marching through all the cities of the German night. Over twenty thousand marched through Hamburg. One woman recorded how the huge crowd of spectators was as if drunk with ecstasy, blinded by torchlight and wreathed in smoke as in a cloud of incense. Next to her in the crowd was a little boy of about three years old. He kept raising his tiny hand and saying "Heil Hitler, Heil Hitlermann".

At that time Barth was lecturing in Bonn on the history of Protestant Theology from the 18th Century. A history with Schleiermacher at the centre, he who more brilliantly than anyone before or since made humanity rather than God the subject of theology, creating that modern theology which revolves forever around the experiences, feelings and awareness of the Christian or, in the case of those who like to appear radical, the non-Christian.

Barth did not have a love-hate relationship with Schleiermacher, rather one of admiration – opposition with both poles felt profoundly. His admiration for Schleiermacher was not only for his undoubted intellectual brilliance but also for his tireless efforts to liberalise the oppressive Prussian State of his time.

Already an eminent author and preacher, translator of Plato into German, Schlierermacher's house in Halle had been plundered and occupied by Napoleon's troops after the defeat of the Prussian Army in 1806. The university he had taught in was closed and his church used by the French as a grain store. When the French dismembered Prussia by giving Halle to Westphalia,

Schleiermacher went to Berlin, now capital of a shrunken Prussia, stripped of all its universities. There he played a major role in creating the University of Berlin, in bringing science and culture to Prussia, and helping to lay the foundations of that German scholarship which in years to come was to evoke both admiration and envy throughout Europe.

On the day following Hitler's triumph Karl Barth wrote to his mother in Switzerland to let her know that he did not see the advent of Hitler as leading to any great novelties in Germany. The country was too sluggish for there to be any great changes and besides, Hitler and his like were only mediocrities. The German people lacked all daring and were simply incapable of producing a German version of such a dangerous character as Mussolini. Events therefore were unlikely to develop in a disquieting way. On the same day he discussed the future of 'Between the Times' with its publisher. Barth was concerned at the attitudes of some of his co-contributors; perhaps the time had come to cease publication rather than run the risk of articles appearing which supported a National Socialist government. He was persuaded to allow the magazine to continue. Despite what he had written to his mother he also began to read 'Mein Kampf' for the first time.

At the beginning of February, Hitler broadcast to the nation. One of the main tasks of his government would be the protection of Christianity as a basis of all morality. He ended his broadcast "May Almighty God take our work to his grace, give true form to our will, bless our insight and endow us with the confidence of our People, for we do not mean to fight for ourselves but for Germany".

A few weeks later the Reichstag building was in flames and to many it was the factual proof that Hitler had been right all along. The torching of the Parliament building, an act which appeared ripe with far-left symbolism, was the first step in a communist plot to destabilise the country, to create uncertainty, then chaos, as a prelude to revolution. There was now held out to many Germans a simple choice: either Hitler and the firm steps he would take to protect the People or the dreary barbarism and unthinking brutality which marked the Soviet Union. How could there be a serious choice for a church presented with such alternatives, only too conscious of the fate of the Orthodox church in Russia and the taunts of the far-left in Germany.

Few in the church considered that it may have been the Nazis themselves who set fire to the Reichstag.

Hitler broadcast again to the whole of the nation, asking for its support. He left no doubt that he was also asking for God's help. "Lord God, may we never become vacillating and cowardly, may we never forget the responsibility we have assumed... we are all proud that by God's gracious help we have again become true Germans". He evoked a genuine response from many in the Church who had not previously yielded to National Socialism. They could now recognise in him more than a simple rabble-rouser, the man of the streets with his following from the slums. He had come not to destroy but to heal; he understood Christian values and would put them into practice.

The message which the Bishops of Holstein and Schleswig gave their communities was typical. "A German Freedom Movement with a national consciousness has emerged from the distress in Germany... The leaders have acknowledged openly that only on a Christian basis can a healthy state develop. This is a change for which we thank God with all our heart".

There were a few dissenters. Early in March Otto Dibelius sent the Pastors of his district a confidential letter. This told of his own delight that, for the first time since the end of the Great War, there was now a government with a consciously nationalist attitude. There would, he was sure, be only a few among his pastors who "do not delight in this change with all their hearts". Then he gave a warning. The church must not be carried away from its true task by a tide of political enthusiasm. "Politics may dig trenches; statesmen may speak of annihilation, extermination and suppression; messages of hate at mass rallies may earn applause that does not want to stop. We have received another spirit... I... will never deviate from the position which the Gospel accords us, and I hope that you will act in the same way. Where hatred is preached, and now even hatred against members of our own people, the spirit of Jesus Christ is not present".

In marking his letter "confidential" Dibelius betrayed his naivety; it was reprinted in full in a national socialist newspaper as an example of treason in the church. A meeting of all the senior members of the Prussian church, including Dibelius, was held to determine what should be the attitude of the Prussian church to the new state. Almost all were in favour of issuing a public message endorsing the new state. One of the arguments in favour of such a move was that the younger generation of pastors especially were in favour of National Socialism. Dibelius alone argued against. At Easter 1933 the millions of Protestant Christians in Prussia heard as the official message of their church:

"This year the Easter Message of the Risen Christ goes forth in a Germany to a People to whom God has spoken by means of a great turning point in history. We know that we are at one with all Protestant fellow believers in joy at the awakening of the deepest powers of our nation to a patriotic consciousness, to a true community of the People, and to a religious renewal".

When Dibelius spoke in his letter of the political preaching of hatred the context would appear to suggest that what he had in mind was the political invective of the Nazis directed against the Social Democrats. But the Social Democrats, and even the Communists, were part of the People and could eventually be persuaded, by one means or another, to see the error of their ways. There were others in Germany however who were not part of the People.

Early in March steps were taken against Jews in important legal positions. On the twelfth of that month a large body of SA Brownshirts forced their way into the Breslau law courts. Crying "Jews Out" they marched through every room, throwing all Jewish judges and lawyers out into the street. A compromise was eventually reached whereby the police guaranteed that the courts could go about their businesses in peace provided the judiciary acknowledged the public desire to stem Jewish influence in the administration of justice. Two days after the Breslau incident the leading national socialist newspaper in Berlin demanded similar action in that city. The newspaper did not spare the sensibilities of its readers in its shocked revelation of what lay behind the facade of the law. "Whereas in Breslau at least the very modest beginnings of a clean-up could be made, in the Berlin courts nothing has yet changed. Anyone entering the lawyers quarters in the Central Justice Ministry will flee from the gigantic room appalled. Not even in the Krakow Ghetto could there be more Jews crawling around". Within a few days the newspaper was able to tell its readers that, due to its exposure action was now being taken and an "iron broom" was sweeping through the Berlin law courts.

Stories began appearing in the foreign press of persecution of Jews in Germany. Firms in Britain and America threatened to boycott the importation of German goods. Hitler then announced that, as a defensive measure, there would be a one-day boycott of Jewish businesses and shops on 1 April 1933. This would, he explained, demonstrate to the Jews that if they continued to abuse German hospitality by spreading lies abroad, they would hurt only themselves. Shortly afterwards, a new law barred Jews from government employment. This legal provision was termed the Aryan Paragraph.

In order that Christians in other countries be informed about what was happening to Jews in Germany the Central Office of the German Evangelical Federation prepared a memorandum which set out both the facts foreigners should be aware of and the position of the church in relation to these matters. This memorandum explained that in the past few months a rebirth had taken place in Germany. The key to this profound upheaval lay in the failure of the Weimar Republic. "The combination of liberal and Marxist ideas which set its stamp on the constitution of post-war Germany did not prove fruitful for political or national life. Above all, it failed to resolve the dangerous social and political tensions which had for so long beset the German people. This disastrous situation is both the ultimate cause for the rise of the National Socialist movement and the supreme challenge which it faces ..."

Marxism, especially in the form of communism, is such an immediate threat to both state and church that the Government rightly made its defeat a high priority. "In the process, of course, the state has had to act with occasional harshness". Given the momentum of national renewal, it is only to be expected that there have been certain acts of violence, including some against Jews, but these are regretted by the government as much as by the church. Besides, these do not begin to compare with the "ghastly and shameful" events of the 1918 Revolution, which the churches outside Germany totally ignored. Unlike what happened in November 1918, the government which has taken power in 1933 is one whose leaders are loyal to Christianity.

The memorandum urged Christians outside Germany to realise "that the real state of affairs can only be understood from within Germany, by those who have suffered together under the previous dispensation ... A broad cross-section of the nation considered that the way in which various Jewish circles regarded the life and death struggle of our nation during the War as ambiguous or even hostile. On top of this came the fact that after the coup d'etat of 1918 the Jews, thanks to their good relations with the Marxist parties, gained for themselves a disproportionately high number of public offices and other important positions in public life. Then ... culturally inferior Jews from the East were able to settle in Germany or even secure German citizenship. Hand in hand with this went the Jewish infiltration of scholarship, journalism and literature, of theatre and film, while in many cases German scholars and artists were pushed into the background". The main concern, however, is not the disproportionate number of Jews in important positions but the realisation that "the Jewish mentality, so evident in literature, theatre and films, was undermining the Christian faith and ethic ... One cannot stress too much the threat to Christian culture in particular which was mounted under the pretext of intellectual freedom ..."

The boycott of Jewish businesses was a consequence of the spreading of propaganda against Germany. "Since it was proved that the propaganda ... had originated with or been energetically promoted by Jewish circles overseas, the Government decided to conduct a boycott of Jewish businessmen in Germany as a counter measure".

As for the continuing role of the church in the 'Jewish question', foreign Christians should take comfort that the Evangelical Federation would be taking an approach very different from that of the atheistic and crypto-marxist Weimar Republic. Previous attempts to deal with this 'question' had failed due to their having "been determined largely by *humanitarian* considerations, rather than evidencing any relationship to the Word of God". The memorandum urges all Christians to follow the lead now being set by National Socialist Germany and to deal with the 'Jewish problem' and related phenomena such as Communism, not with failed humanitarian considerations but from the "depth of the Gospel" and "in the light of the Word of God."

There were other voices but they were few. The seventy-five year old Wilhelm Baron Von Pechmann was one of the leading figures in the Evangelical Federation, once a Munich banker and politically a nationalist and a monarchist. Resolutely and clearly, he spoke out against "the sea of hatred and lies" now engulfing Germany, urging the Evangelical Federation to make a "grave and decisive" statement against the boycott of Jewish businessmen. The church could not keep silent in such an hour.

Agnes Von Zahn-Harnack, the daughter of Adolf Von Harnack, petitioned the Evangelical Federation to speak out in public against the actions being taken against the Jews and which transgressed the highest commandment in Christianity. Such voices were lost in the enthusiasm of national and religious renewal.

Karl Barth's teaching post at Bonn was now under threat. Günther Dehn had already been dismissed (and was to be imprisoned for a while) and a new law governing the civil service was being used to intimidate or remove from their posts many professors who were members of the Social Democrat Party. In March, the SDP informed its members that they should not sacrifice their academic status because of their party membership; in effect, to resign from the SDP while maintaining their convictions in private.

At this, Barth wrote to Bernhard Rust, the National Socialist minister of Cultural Affairs for Prussia. He told Rust that his academic activities would be shaped entirely by the imperatives of theological objectivity and he could not accept the demand to leave the SDP as a condition for the continuation of his teaching position. No good would come from the denial of his political convictions or from the neglect to declare them openly. No good could come from such denial or neglect either for his students, the church or the German people. He was therefore only prepared to continue teaching on the basis of the open recognition of his formal membership of the SDP. Quite amazingly, Rust agreed to Barth's terms. Two months later, the SDP was prohibited by law and completely disbanded. The Rector of Bonn University then demanded directly from Barth how he now stood in relation to the SDP only to be given the lofty reply "I have arranged these things directly with the Minister himself". It was to remain a source of some satisfaction to Barth that he was probably the last member of the Social Democrat Party in Germany.

Such adherence to principle did not, however, stand in the way of Barth presenting the Bonn authorities with proof of his Aryan ancestry, so as not to lose his post under the provisions of the Aryan Paragraph.

CHAPTER 11

Many years later, when the Second World War had ended and the Cold War had begun, Barth was criticised for not denouncing the Soviet Union as he had the Third Reich. Barth replied that he had no need to. The Soviet Union was deeply unattractive, becoming ever more so on closer acquaintance. There was no especial need for him to point this out, there were enough voices in the West doing so already. National Socialism had presented a quite different threat. Whatever the essence of National Socialism, "what made it interesting from the Christian point of view was that it was a spell which had notoriously revealed its power to overwhelm our souls, to persuade us to believe in its lies and to join in its evil doings... We were hypnotised by it as a rabbit by a giant snake. We were in danger of bringing first incense and then the complete sacrifice to it as to a false God..."

Whatever Hitler's long-term objectives for Christianity - and it may well be that he had dreams of eventually banishing Christianity from the soil of the Reich - there is little doubt as to his short-term objective for the Protestant church in Germany. He wanted a church which gave no trouble and would be part of the National Socialist State. In terms of organisational structure this would best be achieved by absorbing the twenty-eight Landeskirchen of the Evangelical Federation into a single Reich Church, headed by a Reich Bishop who was a national socialist. In this way the principles of One People, One Reich, One Führer would be applied to, and embodied within, the church. These ambitions were not unreasonable. The Protestant church was deeply nationalistic and had long identified with the secular rulers of Germany. In 1933 there was an additional factor which appeared to put the matter beyond any doubt. This was a rising demand by growing numbers within the church that the national socialist revolution now under way be recognised as offering the church a unique opportunity to be of real Christian service to the German people.

In April, the Annual Conference of the Faith Movement of German Christians was held in Berlin. Allies of Hossenfelder in the senior levels of the Party ensured that the deliberations and conclusions of the conference were given the widest publicity. Thus it was that the resolutions of the conference came to be addressed to all members of the Evangelical Federation throughout the whole of Germany:

A single Reich Church to embrace all Protestant Christians within a Reich which will one day embrace all German territories lost after 1918;

The introduction of the Führer principle into the Church. This will mean a Reich Bishop for the Reich Church;

The dismissal of all Pastors of "alien blood" by applying the Aryan Paragraph to the Church.

In his closing speech Hossenfelder made plain that a true Christian had the right to oppose and overthrow a church administration that did not acknowledge without reservations the nationalist renewal in Germany. He ended with a challenge: "The goal of the Faith Movement of German Christians is an Evangelical German Reich Church. The State of Adolf Hitler calls upon the church; the church must hear the call".

This call did not go unanswered; it evoked an enthusiastic response throughout the church. Among those calling most vigorously for a matching renewal in the church was Emmanuel Hirsch. "If we in theology and the church do not measure up to this moment, if we are unable to risk giving up all the prejudices stemming from the past and all the need for security and certainty in the boisterous new age, in the vigorous movement of our own People, then we are lost. There is no middle way; there is only the "either/or". Hirsch now joined the German Christians, becoming one of their most senior theological advisers.

The challenge to theology and the church was also put clearly by a young church historian. "The church is asked, not by a party outside or within itself, but rather by history, whether it has the inner strength to interpret a great turning point in German destiny as coming from the hand of God, and to take a creative part in it. If the church ignores this question, or if it does not summon up this power, then despite its best intentions it will *ipso facto* have become a Sect and be condemned to historical impotence. For anyone who does not hear the command to mobilise or who has to stay at home as being unfit for active duty has certainly forfeited the intrinsic right to play a role in German history for the foreseeable future".

The call to interpret a turning point in the destiny of their country as coming from the hand of God and to take a creative part in it was heard by the leading theologians in Germany and among the books which now appeared were:

Paul Althaus - "The German Hour of the Church".

Freidrich Gogarten - "The Unity of the Gospel and the People".

Adolf Schlatter - "The New German Nature in the Church".

Ethelbert Stauffer - "Our Faith and Our History".

Karl Heim - "German State Religion or Protestant Volkskirche".

As Karl Heim wrote in his book, "At the times in which something great occurs in which storms churn up the depth of the sea, out of their inner emptiness and insecurity, human beings always ask after God again. This happened in the Wars of Independence; it happened in August 1914; and so it is happening anew today. There is an open door into which we must enter... We have opportunities present which were not previously there, and which perhaps will never return".

Many years later Barth wrote a commentary on that passage in Exodus in which the Israelites set up and worship the Golden Calf. He writes that in setting up the Golden Calf the Israelites were proclaiming that they had now realised that their God Jehovah was in fact the mystery and essence of themselves as a people. That the holiness of God was the dignity of Israel's humanity, the grace of God the joy of its own fullness of power, the commandment of God the will to live out its own life. It was only right therefore to celebrate, to feast, to make the greatest possible noise and to see the greatest possible enjoyment. Barth adds, "when things have gone so far men do not think .... Of the absurdity of that which they think is their true God – the Calf which is themselves – or the danger into which they plunge themselves with this game". There is little doubt that his experience of Germany in 1933 lies behind this commentary on the worship of the Golden Calf.

Despite his standing as the most prominent and controversial theologian in Germany Karl Barth remained silent however. During the early months of the National Socialist State he made no public comment on the new situation in the country or the developing events in the church. Instead he kept busy lecturing to his students in Bonn. He had also become friendly with the Benedictine Monks at the nearby Maria Laach.

Charlotte von Kirschbaum wrote to Eduard Thurneysen to reassure him that, to her surprise, Barth's teaching work continued to run smoothly and he had good relations with his students despite being vilified publicly by the German Christians. His large and attentive classes included Nazis in full uniform with their caps hanging dutifully on the pegs provided. Barth told his students that for them in 1933 "only quite serious theological work can have any significance".

The Nazi Government arrested so many communist leaders and activists that the jails overflowed and the first concentration camps were established. Stories began to circulate abroad of the treatment of the prisoners in these camps. On behalf of the church in Prussia, Otto Dibelius requested that he be allowed to inspect conditions in one of the camps. Afterwards he made a broadcast to America in which he was able to assure his listeners that, on the basis of his personal inspection of a concentration camp, the "hair-raising news reports about cruel and bloody treatment of the communists in Germany" was untrue. As regards the boycott of Jewish businesses, from what he had observed in his own diocese, it had been conducted "calmly and in order". Americans should also realise that the action taken against Jews in public sector posts had been to rectify the imbalance created under the Weimar Republic whereby Jews had occupied a disproportionate number of senior posts. He concluded by telling his American audience that while the church "cannot and should not hinder the state when it creates order with harsh measures", the church looked forward urgently to the day when such measures were no longer necessary. This day would come all the quicker when "the agitation against Germany ceases in the outside world".

Dibelius was courageous and outspoken, a critic of the Nazi party's language of hate towards fellow-Germans, He did not fear to take a moral stand, believing that Christianity itself is based on moral values. At that time at least, that time of illusions, it was outwith the scope of his moral vision to contemplate that when a senior churchman inspected a concentration camp he would be shown only what the authorities wanted him to see and that a Government of national and religious renewal would use his moral integrity as an instrument in its war of lies.

As the desire voiced by Hossenfelder for a single Reich Church grew more widespread and urgent throughout the church, as the German Christians grew in popularity and influence, so questions and issues began to crystallise. The organisational structure of any Reich Church needed to be clarified; formidable legal hurdles would have to be overcome if the Landeskirchen were to be abolished and incorporated into the Reich Church. If there were first to be appointed a Reich Bishop who would then oversee the work of transforming the Evangelical Federation into a Reich Church then whoever is Reich Bishop will have the future of the Protestant church in Germany in his hands. The various factions and leading personalities within the Evangelical Federation, some seeking power and others seeking to retain the power they already have, began to manoeuvre and take up positions.

Hitler now needed to know what was going on in the church, and who and why, at this critical time. While keeping apart he needed to influence events decisively. He needed his own representative in the Evangelical Federation.

Standing in the bright sunlight Ludwig Müller stares straight at the camera though his eyes are partly hidden in the shadow cast by the brim of the bowler hat set firmly upon his head. Even so there is little doubt that the stare is firm and strong, probably even piercing. The stance is challenging. A tough no-nonsense man he does have some redeeming petty vanities. He wears a fetching black coat, very well fitting, which sets off elegantly the medals, orders and decorations displayed on his chest. Beside him is Prince August Wilhelm of Prussia, who wears a uniform of very superior cut with a dashing cap and a swastika armband. This photograph gratifies three of Ludwig Müller's pleasures: to show off his medals, to be with members of the military, to be with members of the aristocracy.

A naval chaplain during the Great War he had been since military chaplain at Königsberg. Described by a fellow pastor as having a child-like belief and unconditional trust in God, Ludwig Müller was a member of the German Christians, was devoted to Adolf Hitler, and had been a successful propagandist for the Party among the officers of the Königsberg garrison.

On 25th April Hitler announced: "Recent events have made it necessary to determine policy on a number of questions involving the relation of the State to the Evangelical churches. In view of this I nominate as my representative for the affairs of the Evangelical churches, insofar as they touch on these questions, the Chaplain of Königsberg Military Region, Herr Müller. He also has a particular responsibility for furthering all endeavours to create an Evangelical Reich church".

There are some within the Nazi Government who will come to look upon Ludwig Müller as a bungler. Raised out of provincial anonymity by Adolf Hitler his later years will be equally obscure. Even the cause of his death in 1945 is unclear; while some records show it as suicide, these are disputed. As in the photograph however he will stand for a while in the sun, covered with honours, surrounded by uniforms. He will become the first, and also the last, Reich Bishop of the German Evangelical Reich church.

Hitler chose 1st May 1933 as the day of the official inauguration of the Third Reich. That evening an immense rally was held at Templehof Airfield in Berlin. In the centre of the airfield were the disciplined ranks of the brown-uniformed SA and the black uniformed SS. Gigantic banners waived swastikas over the dignitaries of the new Reich as they made their speeches to the vast and enthusiastic crowd.

For Emmanuel Hirsch the experience of 1 May 1933 was uplifting. "No other People in the world has a leading statesman such as ours, who takes Christianity so seriously. On 1May when Hitler closed his speech with a prayer, the whole world could sense the wonderful sincerity in that". Gertrude Staewen was also there. By then she had divorced and was supporting two small children through a series of ill-paid jobs. She had also written two books; one an oral history of working class women in Berlin. Both were now banned by the Government and some of her friends were already in Gestapo prisons.

Even fifty years later she could vividly recall the dread she felt at Templehof, a sense of the horror and terror to come. "And the Templehof field was filled to the last place with jubilant, screaming people. Only our group sat there and wept. Everyone else was simply enraptured. Then, as it began to get dark, he came. He was carried on the shoulders of the SS men and others held on to his hands. He was carried right through the masses of people, who cheered him and kissed his feet and - he came right by me. That one time in my life I saw him and I knew, Germany is now dead, forever".

CHAPTER 12

The Faith Movement of German Christians is opposed by the existing Federation leadership of the twenty-eight Landeskirchen. Patriotic and loyal they may be but they have come to enjoy the freedom from state control they exercised under the despised Weimar Republic. They do not trust the German Christians. While the existing leadership welcomed the National Socialist State and now welcomes the establishment of a Reich Church, the church must remain independent; an enthusiastic and loyal partner of the state but not part of it. Were the German Christians to triumph in the church they fear the church would lose its independence. These fears deepen when the German Christians nominate Ludvig Müller as their candidate for the post of Reich Bishop. They deepen further when Müller announces that, as National Socialism has conquered the state, so will the Faith Movement of German Christians conquer the church.

Also opposed to the German Christians is the Young Reformation Movement. The reformers see the Evangelical Federation as a church in decay composed of reactionary Landeskirchen. Swift and comprehensive reforms are needed and a unique opportunity is being offered to the church to serve the German people. The Young Reformers demand "that in joyful affirmation of the new German state, the Protestant church should fulfil, in full freedom from all political influence, the mission given it by God and at the same time bind itself in service to the German people". In order to carry out this service the Young Reformers recognise there must be a Reich church, but a church which must remain free from the state. As a demonstration of that freedom the Young Reformation Movement rejects the call by the German Christians that the Aryan paragraph be applied in the church. The Young Reformation Movement has wide appeal and many theologians join, including Friedrich Gogarten.

In the midst of confusion and muddle, with much bad temper and frantic political manoeuvring, the leadership of the Evangelical Federation reject Ludvig Müller as Bishop-elect of the proposed Reich church and instead choose the highly respected pastor Freidrich Von Bodelschwing. That evening Ludvig Müller broadcasts on Berlin radio; his target is the Federation leadership. "You have not heard the voice of God which, through the movement in our People, calls us to daring action .... the Reich

Bishop ought to be a man whose name arouses a response in our fighting groups, a man whom the whole awakening People looks on with trust with all its heart. He ought to be the church's leader for a new birth and a new energy".

The German Christians mobilise all their resources and from pulpits and in meeting-halls all over Germany there are now demands for the spiritual co-ordination of church and state. Emanuel Hirsch is heard demanding an independent church, but a church bound spiritually to the German People. Across the Reich people are urged to speak out against the Federation leadership. Nazi Party members are invited to send telegrams of protest, there are protest rallies. In Lübeck alone twelve separate campaigns are mounted against the Federation leadership, one of which is an open-air rally of 2000 people. In the face of a tide of orchestrated public protest throughout Germany Bodelschwing is forced to resign.

On the day Bodelschwing fell, the Party, in the form of the Prussian Ministry of Culture, also moved in support of the German Christians. Exploiting a legal technicality, a commissioner is appointed to take over the administration of the Old Prussian Union. This commissioner was August Jäger, a lawyer who immediately placed the Prussian Church under police jurisdiction. A number of pastors were sacked, others suspended or arrested. Among those suspended was Otto Dibelius. In times to come, August Jäger was to work closely with Müller and the German Christians, displaying the capacity for swift and even violent action which marked those eager to exercise leadership in the new Reich. Seven years later the outbreak of war and invasion of Poland provided even greater opportunities and Jäger became one of the most powerful men in the German administration of occupied Poland. After the defeat of the Third Reich, he stood before a Polish Court accused of war crimes and crimes against humanity including the mass murder of civilians and prisoners. He was found guilty and executed in June 1948 despite a plea for clemency from Otto Dibelius.

What for some was a passionate struggle for the soul of the church was for others a needless quarrel tearing apart one of the main pillars of national life. For the only time during Hitler's chancellorship, President Hindenburg, held in revered awe by much of Germany, used the press to make his views known to the whole nation. Under banner headlines, Germans could read the text of a letter their President, national hero and Field Marshall, had just sent to his Chancellor and ex-corporal "As a Protestant

Christian and supreme head of the nation", began Hindenburg, setting his lion's paw on both his church and his Chancellor. From the volume of representations made to him, it was evident the ordinary members of the church were "deeply disturbed by these confrontations and by concern for the internal freedom of the church. A continuation or intensification of this situation can only bring the most grievious harm to People and Fatherland". He was however confident that his Chancellor was ready to play his part and, with his vision and statesmanship, would bring about peace between the warring factions in the church.

A hastily convened meeting between Hitler, Ludvig Müller, and the Reich officials responsible for church affairs was understandably fraught. Eventually a strategy was agreed.

First, elections for new governing bodies of the church at local level will be held in July. The new governing bodies will nominate delegates to a National Synod which will then elect a Reich Bishop who with the help of that Synod, will complete the union of the twenty-eight Landeskirchen into a single Reich Church. The crucial element, which will determine all that follows, will be the outcome of the church elections. To assist the German Christian election campaign, a set of new guidelines for the Movement is prepared. These are in large parts drawn up by Emanuel Hirsch and approved not only by Müller but also by Hitler.

Freidrich Gogarten, following his intention of being sensitive to the traces of God's action in history and seeking to find Christ in his neighbour, now joined the German Christians. He explained that it was the National Socialist state which had created the necessary preconditions for "the unhindered proclamation of the risen Lord, crucified for our sins, to fall upon productive soil".

Barth told George Mertz, still editor of "Between the Times", that he could no longer contribute to the magazine. There needed to be a complete break between him and Gogarten and also some of the other contributors to the magazine who thought like Gogarten. With Barth's withdrawal the magazine ceased publication. The time between the times had come to an end amid bitterness and recrimination; some personal wounds were opened which were never to be healed.

So far Hitler had never needed to intervene directly in the affairs of the church. He knew what he wanted and others sought to achieve it for him. It was therefore without precedent when the day before the church elections he broadcast to the nation "in making clear what my position is in regard to the Evangelical church elections, I am acting purely in my capacity as the political Führer; in other words, the questions of faith, dogmatics and doctrine are no concern of mine. These are entirely internal church matters. But apart from them, there are problems which compel the political and responsible Führer of the People to make his position clear .... since the state, after all, is prepared to guarantee the inner freedom of religious life, it had a right to hope that within the confessions, those forces will gain a hearing which are resolutely determined to make their own contribution to the freedom of the nation. This latter, however, will not be brought about by the unrealistic forces of religious ossification - unable to grasp the importance of contemporary phenomena and events - but only by the enthusiasm of a dynamic movement. This enthusiasm appears to me to be located primarily in that part of the Protestant population which has set itself firmly on the basis of the National Socialist state - the German Christians". On the following day, the German Christians win three quarters of the votes in the church elections and take control of the Protestant church in Germany. Among the few opponents of the German Christians who were successful in these elections was Charlotte von Kirschbaum.

The spirit of a church in harmony with its times is shown at the first meeting of the Prussian Synod, the governing body of the Old Prussian Union. The German Christian majority are in full uniform. Brownshirts, black riding boots, leather waist and shoulder straps, swastika armbands. Some with medals and badges of rank. New laws for the Old Prussian Union are voted through with large majorities. One of the first concerns the Aryan paragraph. "Anyone who is of non-Aryan extraction, or is married to a person of non-Aryan extraction may not be called as a minister or official in the general church administration. Who is to be considered a person of non-Aryan extraction is determined by the prescriptions of the Reich law." This new law applies to those already in post. Attempts by the opposition to speak against the motions are shouted down. The day ends with an address by Ludvig Müller encouraging the Synod in its further work. "In all your labours and all your desires, always look beyond what is past to the Everlasting and the Eternal".

As the German Christians triumph in the summer and autumn of 1933 a religious revival takes place in the church. While the church had weathered the atheist storm and survived the godless years of the Weimar Republic, church leaders had been concerned at the drift of people away from the church. Now, however, the People were coming back to a People's church. In Thuringia nine times as many people joined in 1933 as had in 1932. In Bavaria admissions doubled. There were now mass weddings and baptisms and in one church in Berlin thirty four couples are married at the same time, and in another one hundred and seventeen children are given a mass baptism. One church reports at Harvest Festival that there had never been so many people in the church for fifteen years and even so there were still four hundred outside who could not get in.

In September comes the climax of that summer of struggle for the church. The first meeting of the National Synod and election by the Synod of the Reich Bishop. The National Synod is held in Wittenberg, Luther's own city. Hugh crowds are in the streets and from the buildings are draped swastika banners. A German Christian magazine describes the scene in inimitable fashion "and then dawns the day 27 September 1933! A splendid sun again smiles from the cloudless sky, and the bells ring festively and ceremonially. All of Wittenberg is on its feet. Shortly after 11 o'clock the huge procession starts to move to the Stadtkirche; flags of the SA storm groups from Wittenberg, the flags of the Protestant youth organisations, of the craft guilds, of the associations; the theological faculties in festive robes, the clergy of Luther's city in gowns, the members of the senate, the Lutherans in brownshirts, the Bishops of the German Landeskirchen with the golden pectoral crosses of their office and - the man who all eyes seek in awe, inquiringly and full of hope: the future Reich Bishop, Ludwig Müller".

During the church service, the attention of the congregation is understandably diverted from both Ludvig Müller and the solemn proceedings by the fascinating spectacle of a little novelty devised by the Bishop of Saxony. He has transformed his theological students into storm troopers with field grey uniforms and jack boots, with heavy field packs on their backs, with bread bags and water flasks and with a purple cross which sets off the SS flashes on their arms.

After the proceedings, the service over, the spokesman for the National Synod announces "Ludwig Müller has been elected Reich Bishop unanimously.... Protestant Germany has its Führer".

Then Ludwig Müller makes a speech, quite courteous. He ends "the old is ending, the new is dawning. The church's political struggle is over. The struggle for the soul of the People is beginning".

As he leaves the Stadtkirche, coming out of the darkness into the sunlight, he pauses at the top of the steps. On either side of him, crowding the large doorway behind him, lining either side of the flights of steps are masses of uniformed men and banners, and they and the waiting crowd join him as he throws up his hand in the Hitler salute. In the evening there are again huge crowds and a torchlight procession through the streets.

The fury of the church struggle had left little time for theological debate. The triumph of the German Christians, and the utter failure of their opponents, had been based upon church political considerations. The events which were now to follow were based increasingly upon theological considerations.

At the beginning of July there appeared Karl Barth's "Theological Existence Today". This small book had been written virtually at a single sitting during the evening and night of the day on which Bodelschwing fell and Prussian State Commissioner Jäger had taken over administration of the Prussian Church. It began: "For a good while back I have been frequently asked if I have nothing to say about the concerns and problems affecting the German Church nowadays. I can no longer ignore these requests coming as they do from many of my former pupils and others who share my theological outlook. But I must at once make clear that the essence of what I attempt to contribute today, bearing upon these anxieties and problems, cannot be made the theme of a particular manifesto for the simple reason that at Bonn here with my students and lectures and courses, I endeavour to carry on theology and only theology, now as previously and as if nothing had happened. Perhaps there is a slightly increased tone but without direct allusions: Something like the chanting of the hours by the Benedictines nearby in the Maria Laach, which goes on undoubtedly without break or interruption, pursuing the even tenor of its ways even in the Third Reich".

CHAPTER 13

On March 10 1933, a few days after the Reichstag fire Barth had given a lecture in Copenhagen on "The First Commandment as a Theologoical Axiom".

"Theology is an attempt by means of human thought and speech to achieve scientific clarity on the question of the church's basis, law, and proclamation. From the very first, then, it stands in the sphere of Scripture and the first commandment. Where axioms stand in other sciences, in theology – before all theological thought or speech –there stands at the source or root, basic and critical, though in a way different from that of other axioms, the command: "Thou shalt have no other gods but me" (Ex. 20:3). Theologically, I think and speak responsibly when in my thinking and speaking I know that I am responsible to this command, and when I see in this responsibility the accountability to a court from which there can be no appeal because it is the last and supreme court and absolutely decisive. "Thou shalt have no other gods but me." Nothing is less self-evident than that theology should have no other gods alongside the God of the church. It is as little self-evident today as it was at Sinai, or on the morning that Jesus Christ rose from the dead, that his God rises up and makes himself heard – "I am the Lord thy God" – and makes other gods as nothing, and takes our hearts captive so that we have to fear *him* and trust *him*. Theology too, and it precisely, is always questioned where its heart and concerns and interests really lie, and whether its heart is secretly divided between this God and other gods."

All theologies have other Gods than the God who prohibits the creation of other Gods. These Gods are most clearly seen when theology believes there are authorities and concepts it must regard as binding. Examples in that year 1933 are "religious experience", "state", "people" or "history".

When the church or theology speak of these other authorities and concepts they must recognise the responsibility demanded by the first commandment. "This responsibility will be demonstrated in the fact that it will interpret those other authorities by the criterion of revelation and not interpret revelation by the criterion of those other authorities. It will not seek to investigate heaven with a search light set up on earth, but rather will attempt to see and to understand the earth in the light of heaven.... In any case there will be no possibility whatsoever of the mixing or exchange, no possibility of an identification" of the created with the divine. Protestantism has not recognised this responsibility in a clear way since the time of Schleiermacher.

In 'Theological Existence Today' Barth therefore could describe the German Christians not as deviants but as only too representative of Protestant thinking.

The German Christians were simply pointing out that their particular ideas and ideals were relevant to the times and should therefore be used by the church for the proclamation of the Gospel, which in itself, of course, would remain unaltered. "Exactly the same thing had happened at the beginning of the Eighteenth Century with the reviving humanism ... with idealism ... with romanticism ... with the bourgeois society and scholarship of the Nineteenth Century, and the nationalism of the same period, and a little later socialism ... and there were so many parallels to it that no one outside really had the right to cast a stone at Germany because the new combination there involved the combination with race nationalism which happened to be rather uncongenial to the rest of the world ... Now that so many other combinations had been allowed to pass uncontradicted, and had even been affectionately nurtured, it was about two hundred years too late to make any well-founded objections". No matter how crude and unacceptable, the German Christians were the heirs of Schliermacher's legacy. This is where our supposed religious awareness, able to sense intimations of the divine in nature or events or our consciousness, has led us. Here is the synthesis of religion and society.

At the beginning of 'Theological Existence Today' Barth listed the events happening at the very time on which he wrote. The appointment by the state of a commissioner to take over the administration of the church in Prussia; the removal of church officials; the take-over of the church press bureau by the German Christians, and the fall of Bodelschwing as provisional Reich Bishop. Despite such events he explains it is imperative that he continue doing theology "as if nothing has happened". Theologians must continue their existence as theologians and not abandon that task for another they think preferable. It is not wrong to be a politician but that is quite different from being a theologian. When the church acts, or does not act, its actions or inactions have political consequences. Such decisions, however, must be derived not from political insights or analogies but from the confessing of its faith.

On all sides Barth sees the confusion which results when the church abandons theological reflection and puts its trust in church political action or parallels drawn from the sphere of current politics. There is, for example, the issue of the Reich Bishop. All sides of the church struggle have agreed on the need for a Reich Bishop but where does this need come from, this need which is now so urgent but was within no ones mind before 1933? Not from any internal necessity of the church. The clamour of the necessity for a Reich Bishop, a leader of the church, is the church simply echoing the dominant political trend in the world around it. As for what kind of Reich Bishop, what kind of leader, the church can have in mind in the Germany of 1933. Surely it can only be "the principle of leadership as seen in the concrete form of Adolf Hitler".

While what the German Christians have to say is derived from the scrapings of various theological dustbins their doctrine is none the less dangerous for all that. The church "ought rather to become a tiny group and go into the catacombs than sign a peace, even covertly, with this doctrine... The Church... does not believe in any state, therefore not even in the German one... The Church teaches the Gospel in all the kingdoms of the world, she preaches it also *in* the Third Reich but not *under* it nor in *its* spirit". As for the fellowship of the Church it is not determined by blood. If the Protestant Church in Germany "excludes Jewish-Christians, or treats them as of a lower grade, she ceases to be a Christian Church".

Barth does not deny some merit to the German Christians; they have at least revealed the true nature of the church in Germany. All those terribly important and significant and apparently opposing groups which make up the church, what can be said of them now? Bishops and ordinary church members; professors and students; educated and illiterate; young and old; liberals and fundamentalists; Lutherans and Calvinists. Now united as one in their utter lack of effective resistance to the call of the German Christians, surrendering in droves at the noise of this movement, at the cries of "Revolution, Reality, Life, Mastery or Destiny". There is no fundamental opposition to the German Christians not even from the members of the Young Reformation Movement. They may reject the Aryan paragraph, and this rejection is to be praised, but they are utterly compromised by their joyous assent on behalf of the church, to the new German state. By such joyous assent they display that they are not, at root, sufficiently distinct from the German Christians.

At the end Barth sets out, in a few words, his own call to the church.

"All that is called Liberty, Justice, Spirit only a year ago and for one hundred years further back, where has it all gone? Now these are all temporal, material, earthly goods, "all flesh is as the grass". No doubt! There is no doubt that many people in olden times, and later, have had to do without these preferred goods and have been able to, if the bold enterprise of the Totalitarian State demands it of them. "But the Word of our God abideth forever", and consequently, it is true and indispensable every day; for ever day hastens into Eternity. Because of this theology and the Church cannot enter upon a winter sleep within the Total State; no moratorium and no "assimilation" can befall them. They are the natural frontiers of everything even the Totalitarian State. For even in this Total State the nation always lives by the word of God, the content of which is "forgiveness of sins, resurrection of the body, and life everlasting". To this word the Church and theology have to render service to the people... because of this Church and theology are the frontiers, the bounds, of the State. They are this for the salvation of the people: *That* salvation which neither the State nor yet the Church can create, but which the Church is called upon to proclaim".

When Barth's mother in Switzerland had heard that he was to publish his views on the church struggle she had been concerned for his safety. Charlotte von Kirschbaum wrote assuring her that Barth was taking a position "only as a theologian"; he would abstain from all political statements. The political significance of "Theological Existence Today" was, however, fully appreciated by its enemies. The leading German Christian theologian in Hamburg explained quite correctly that thinking out Barth's position to the end would mean a direct path into a concentration camp. Emmanuel Hirsch responded with all of his usual heartfelt passion. Barth would not be so blind about the church and the People "if he were a German from top to toe like us. If he had experienced as his own, the fate of our People in war and defeat and self-alienation and the national socialist revolution in the way we did, with trembling and joy".

Throughout Germany, in pastor's studies, students' lodgings, workers' flats, this little book came to many as a breath of sharp but fresh air, a new clear note amidst the babble in the

Church, a remembrance of something forgotten.   Thirty four thousand copies of the book were bought before it was banned.

There is no record of Adolf Hitler having commented on the copy which Barth personally sent to him.

CHAPTER 14

In Berlin a month after Ludwig Müller has been elected Reich Bishop there is a Reformation Festival and groups opposed to the German Christians invited Barth to give a lecture. His lecture is entitled "The Reformation as Decision" and is given in the Great Hall of the Berlin Singakadamie which is filled to overflowing. Anyone who celebrates Luther today, he tells his audience, must do so with a sword in his hand. He tells of a decision made at the time of the Reformation. A decision very different from that popular today when people choose faith as a possibility alongside other possibilities such as morality, culture and state. So we choose from among these possibilities and end up with more than one, as for example in "Gospel and People". There is now dominant in the Protestant church a movement which, by choosing such possibilities, betrays every claim to be a church of the Reformation decision. In the name of the true Reformation church, Barth urges his audience to offer the false church only one thing - resistance. At the word "resistance" the cheers are so loud and prolonged he cannot speak for several minutes.

He was now to meet an unlikely ally. In 1918 the captain of the submarine "UC67" refused to stop fighting until he had been convinced that the Kaiser had indeed surrendered. In September 1939, on the outbreak of the Second World War, and in his third year as a prisoner in Sachsenhausen concentration camp, he asked permission to be released so that he could fight the enemies of his Fatherland. Martin Niemöller had determination and courage to an exceptional degree. After a highly decorated career in the Great War, he had practically starved himself so as to complete his theological studies and since 1931 had been a pastor in the Old Prussian Union. Following the election of Ludvig Müller as Reich Bishop, Niemöller had been one of the founders of the Pastors' Emergency League, based on the failed Young Reformation Movement. Members of the League pledged to support religious freedom from state interference and to oppose the imposition of the Aryan paragraph in the church. By the middle of October 1933 the Pastors' Emergency League claimed to have up to three thousand members with Niemöller emerging as moral leader.

When he first met Niemöller in late 1933 Barth's initial reaction was "How Prussian". He distrusted Niemöller, suspecting that his real ambition was to supplant Ludvig Müller as Reich Bishop. One meeting of the League he described as little more than "an ant hill of agitated pastors ready for action under the dictatorship of U Boat Captain Niemöller". Barth considered Niemöller both arrogant and aggressive. Despite these similarities the two men were to become close friends and allies.

Allies were necessary as the opposition to Müller and the German Christians had multiple and deep fractures within itself. Only the Landeskirchen of Bavaria, Wittenberg and Hanover had not fallen to the German Christians in the church elections; the principal objective of the Bishops of these three Landeskirchen being to resist absorption into a state-controlled Reich Church. These three Landeskirchen were called the "intact churches". The attitude of the three Bishops to the Pastors' Emergency League was ambivalent, distrustful as they were of Niemöller's aggressive style and fearful of what he might provoke. As for Karl Barth, they had little or no time for him and relations between him and Bishop Marahrens of Hanover reflected a mutual distaste.

During the autumn of 1933 Barth had a number of meetings in Berlin with members of the League. He made clear he was not urging political resistance to Müller or the German Christians or the national socialist state. For the church, any grounds of resistance must be theological. At a discussion with a large number of League members, Barth emphasised that to give politics priority is a form of captivity for the church. A church which is fully free from politics may, for example, agree at times with what Dr Goebbels says, at other times may disagree. There are times when theological speech may take the form of simply asking questions and he gives some examples. What happened this summer in Germany? Did it happen justly or unjustly? This kind of seizure of power? This elimination of other parties? This confiscation of property? What is happening in the concentration camps? Can Germany, can the German church, explain the volume of suicides? Does not the church share the guilt in this because it is silent?

"I'm only asking questions", Barth said. It was unlikely that anyone else was asking such questions before a gathering of one hundred and fifty people, either in Berlin or anywhere else in Germany. Such talk could be dangerous even in one's own home. Rumour had it that the secret police were everywhere. In this case rumour was quite true. One of those listening to Barth at this meeting was an informer for the Gestapo.

It was at this meeting that Barth first raised the question of a Confession; that step so prominent of the Reformation. A declaration of faith whose public confession marks those confessing as the true church.

"If our attitude", he said to his crowd of listeners (and at least one informer) "to the present church government is such that we have to perceive it as a heretical and illegitimate church government, then our attitude must be that of Paul to Nero. It is well known he did not become a Roman Senator. For anyone who sees things in this way, I see no other possibility than that of those who take their stand on the basis of the confession will confront heresy by coming together in a free synod. There will be no more talk of "brotherhood" and "circle", but you will know that you are there as the legitimate representatives of the true German church".

On the suggestion that such a Confession be prepared and agreed to there and then, Barth quickly backed away. At this time, he explained, such a step would be merely a gesture, nothing more. When the time was ready the church would know, but the time was not yet.

He returned to Bonn dissatisfied with his meetings with the Pastors' Emergency League in Berlin. They put too much trust, he felt, in their ability to oust Ludvig Müller by church-political manoeuvrings; they harboured too many illusions. Despite what he had said about the time not being ripe for a Confession, he began to prepare one. If it is the Holy Spirit which moves the church and tells it when the time is right, he at least was not going to be caught unprepared.

Among those who laboured under an illusion concerning Adolf Hitler were the German Christians. They believed that Adolf Hitler, the Nazi Party and the Faith Movement of German Christians were tied together "with a thousand unbreakable strings". They were mistaken and their trust misplaced. Hitler had supported them in the church elections only as a step towards the creation of a Reich Church in his own image. Ludvig Müller was now Reich Bishop, now taking the necessary steps to legally establish the Reich Church. Legal steps enforced, where necessary, with efficient intimidation.

Even more to the point there was disturbing talk that to be a good National Socialist you were expected to be a German Christian; that had to cease, as it identified Hitler with one faction within one Church. He had to be seen to be above all disputes between or within the Churches. His opportunity came with stories that pastors who were National Socialists but were not German Christians were likely to be dismissed. This presented an opportunity to demonstrate that National Socialism was above religious disputes. On 17 October his deputy Rudolph Hess issued a regulation to the Party.

"No National Socialist may be discriminated against in any way for not adhering to a particular type of belief. Belief is an individual, absolutely personal affair for which one is responsible only to one's own conscience. No pressure may be brought to bear in matters of conscience".

In fact the position of the German Christians had always been somewhat precarious. Threatened by the indifference of large numbers of the population to any form of Christianity, their particular stance brought its own dangers. Seeking popularity and influence by grafting the cross on to the swastika earned only the contempt and resentment of non-Christians in the senior ranks of the Party. Attacking their opponents in the Evangelical Federation as tainted with Judaism brought charges of hypocrisy. Among those making such charges was Jakob Hauer who cheerfully lumped both the German Christians and their church opponents together as sharing an ineradicable Jewish origin alien to German spirituality. Trained as a Protestant pastor, Hauer had been sent to India in 1906 by the Basel Mission. This missionary endeavour was highly successful in a reverse sense in that when Hauer returned to Europe he applied the insights of the Indian religions and philosophy to Christianity. Becoming Professor of Indian Studies and Comparative Religion at the University of Tübingen he blended Nordic and Indian symbols and text to advocate the superiority of Aryan religions over the Semitic. The movement he established gained forty thousand members, a strong position from which to harry the German Christians for being insufficiently radical.

Despite their differences there was one feature the German Christians shared with all other Christian churches; sex was a problem. The particular problem for the German Christians arose from their belief that in this world only the strong will survive so real men must lead the way, strong manly heroic men just like Jesus while back in the kitchen their women will be cooking their dinner in between breeding more strong manly, etc.

Unfortunately women not only made up a large part of the German Christian membership they were in general more active than the men and the movement was entirely dependent on their energy. Hauer's rival movement had no such weakness; he considered women superior to men in spiritual intuition. In their struggle with their church opponents on one side and rival movements such as Hauer's on the other the German Christians had however a powerful weapon denied to the others. This was their outspoken and hard-hitting magazine "The Gospel in the Third Reich". Both Müller and the German Christian leadership always kept very very quiet that its editor was a Miss Wiedermann.

As in most movements the German Christians have their radicals, their conservatives and those who hope they will never have to declare for either. The radicals were impatient to complete the revolution in the church. They were also concerned at the grossly liberal tone of Hess' instruction. This was not what they had come to expect from the Party. It was time to demonstrate that in all of Germany there were no truer National Socialists than the German Christians; that of all people, they were most in harmony with the Führer's deepest aspirations. The national rally of the German Christians in the Berlin Sports Palace in November gave the opportunity they desired.

The community groups of the German Christians march in with banners aloft, filling up all 20,000 seats of the huge hall. On the platform sits Hossenfelder, the national leader, Dr Krause, the Berlin leader and other dignitaries. They are in full uniform, with riding boots and swastika armbands. From the tiers of packed balconies huge swastika flags looked down.

The opening ceremonies completed, Hossenfelder leaves early; he has a Nuremberg Rally the next day. Now Dr Krause has the audience to himself. As is usual in such gatherings the audience is mainly composed of activists and radicals. Dr Krause too is a radical and the decisive moment for the Faith Movement of German Christians has arrived.

We have One People and One Führer, declares Krause, but not yet One church. Now is the time for the Movement to decide what kind of church it wants. Whether the old discredited, reactionary and authoritarian one, or a new, genuine church of the German People. He sets out his own vision of such a church.

"The first priority is to win over the flood of those who are returning to the church. This requires liberation from the Old Testament with its Jewish recompense ethic, from all those stories about cattle-dealers and pimps. This book has been characterised quite rightly as one of the most questionable books in the world's history ... If we national socialists are ashamed to buy a tie from a Jew we should be even more ashamed to accept from Jews something of central religious importance that speaks to our souls".

He demands that "superstitious reports should be expunged from the New Testament and that the whole scape-goat and inferiority-type theology of the Rabbi Paul should be renounced in principle for it has perpetrated a falsification of the Gospel, of the simple message: "Love your neighbour as yourself" - regard your neighbour as your brother and God as your father. The fact is that ... theology from Paul to Barth has made a speculative exercise out of our God-Father". Paul and Barth have tried to separate God and man, but the pure teaching of Jesus knows no such separation except when man deliberately sets himself apart from God. This is the pure teaching which must again become the foundation of the Church. "When we draw from the Gospel that which speaks to our German hearts, then the essentials of the teachings of Jesus clearly and revealingly emerge, coinciding completely with the demands of national socialism - and of that we may be proud". The Third Reich needs men, not slaves. Exaggerated presentations of the crucified Jesus must go. "And we will experience how close is the relationship of the Nordic spirit to the heroic spirit of Jesus. Then it will be clear that the fulfilment of Martin Luther's reformation means a final victory of Nordic spirit over Eastern materialism. Heil!"

When he finishes the almost frantic applause goes on and on. For the radicals among the German Christians in the hall it must have seemed that their hour had come. Perhaps there had been moments when Dr Artur Dinter had felt the same way.

The great wave of exultation surging around the Sports Palace was not the sound of the German Christian triumph but of their fall. From the pulpits of the Pastors' Emergency League came the accusation that Krause had denied the truth of holy scripture and insulted Christ. The congregations of the League were reminded of Christ's warning in Matthew's Gospel "But whosoever shall deny me before men, him will I also deny before my Father which is in heaven". A swell of opposition mounted against the German Christians and membership of the League leapt to 7,000, half the active pastors in Germany. The three intact Churches buried their differences with the League to form a united front and the church opposition became almost overnight the most powerful group in the Protestant church.

As the church opposition grew in strength, the Faith Movement of German Christians began to disintegrate. Krause was suspended, then expelled. Some of the more moderate German Christians then entered a loose alliance with the church opposition. There were large defections from the Movement, including Friedrich Gogarten and the group of theologians associated with him.

One of the original groups which had led to the formation of the German Christians was that led in Thuringia by Leffler and Leutheuser. They saw Hossenfelder's distancing of the leadership from radicals such as Krause as the triumph of expediency over spiritual principle. Leffler's letter to Hossenfelder brims with anger and contempt at the betrayal of a reforming movement by a leadership more interested in position than principle. "You have thrown out the former church rulers. Certainly that was necessary. And you and your Berlin friends have occupied Dioceses and Bishops thrones instead. But truly you have not achieved more than that. You have turned the good idea of German Christianity into a matter of church politics". The spirit of Christ lay elsewhere. As Leutheuser explained "Hitler has brought Christ to us", it was Hitler who was "the spokesman for a Saviour who wills to be, and indeed has become, flesh and blood in the German People". In National Socialism "there is already the new body of Christ". Ten years later, on the eve of his death on the Eastern Front he could still say: "the Fuhrer means he who has led us to God and People".

Unable to satisfy all sides, or even one side, Ludwig Müller was becoming increasingly isolated. There were however those who stood by him. Emmanuel Hirsch assured Müller: "I believe that what I perceive your path and intention to be are definite for me, so I am staying with the German Christians... I am glad to run the risk of being called a heretic. My feeling is simple; I *do not abandon our standard when the bombardment becomes heavy*". There were no doubt some who considered this metaphor somewhat unfortunate given that during the Great War Hirsch had been rejected for military service as being physically unfit.

Throughout the whole church new alliances are formed, old friendships reassessed, there is much bustling to seize initiatives. Müller hints that he may have to call in the Gestapo to restore order. The Gestapo reports, in secret of course, that it has lost track of what is happening in the church. Müller acts to end the confusion and restore his authority. In December he abolishes the Church Youth Organisation; boys transferred to the Hitler Youth, girls to the League of German Maidens. In January he issues a directive enforcing the Aryan Paragraph throughout the Church and prohibiting any criticism of himself. When the Pastors' Emergence League denounces these actions Müller retaliates with suspensions, dismissals, and in some cases with arrests. Müller is engulfed in condemnation; some in the Government are starting to regard him as a fool and Hindenberg lets it be known that he favours the church opposition. The church struggle is now starting to threaten the fabric of the National Socialist State.

Then Adolf Hitler announces that he is willing to use his good offices as Chancellor to help resolve the conflict, and invites representatives of all factions to a meeting with him at the Chancellery on 25th January. The eagerness and hope with which this invitation is accepted on all sides, the trust that he alone can heal their divisions, reveals that in a very real sense he has become Führer of the Protestant church in Germany.

CHAPTER 15

While the Pastors' Emergence League opposed the application of the Aryan paragraph in the church, this opposition had little or nothing to do with combating anti-semitism. Application of the Aryan paragraph in the church restricted the church's freedom to regulate its own affairs, to make its own appointments. Opposition to the Aryan paragraph arose primarily out of concern for the independence of the church not for the fate of individual Jews.

Barth was therefore somewhat out of step even with the majority of the church opposition when, in December 1933 in one of his rare sermons at that time he called for clear recognition that "Jesus Christ was a Jew". At this, some of his own congregation left the church in protest. Afterwards, he wrote to one of the congregation explaining that "anyone who believes in Christ, who was himself a Jew, and died for Gentiles and Jews *simply cannot* be involved in the contempt for Jews and ill-treatment of them which is now the order of the day". What he did not say was that he did not actually like Jews. Only many years later, towards the end of his life did he admit that Jews made him uncomfortable. "In personal encounters with living Jews (even Jewish Christians), I have always, so long as I can remember, had to suppress a totally irrational aversion, naturally suppressing it at once on the basis of all my beliefs and positions, and concealing it totally in my statements, yet still have to suppress and conceal it. Pfui! is all I can say to this in some sense allergic reaction of mine. But this is how it was and is".

Karl Barth was a man of many faults, some deep, but paying any attention or ascribing any importance whatsoever to his "allergic reaction" was not one of them. To one of his listeners who was troubled about her Jewish relatives he explained "Through faith in Christ who Himself was a Jew ... we cannot simply refrain from joining in the disdain and maltreatment of the Jews which is on today's agenda ... We certainly may not join in here, not even in our thoughts, nor out of thoughtlessness, nor out of fear of men, particularly those in power, and also not for some outward advantages or disadvantages. To repeat: we may not"

In December 1938, after he had left Germany and only a few weeks after Kristallnacht he declared at a conference –

"... National Socialism is basically the anti-Christian, counter-church. Hitler and others who may be particularly responsible for National Socialist anti-Semitism, of course, have no idea what they have stirred up here ... Whenever this happens ...: precisely the "physical extermination" of the people of Israel, precisely [the] burning of the synagogues and the Torah-scrolls, precisely the rejection of the "God of the Jews" and the "Bible of the Jews" – as the embodiment of all that should be a horror to the German people, with all these things and if only the things that have taken place *already* – a decision is made; the Christian Church is attacked here at its root and an attempt is made to kill it off ... Whoever is, in principle, an enemy of Jews, is as such – even if he happens to appear as an angel of light – is, in principle, an enemy of Jesus Christ. Anti-Semitism is sin against the Holy Spirit... And it is precisely in anti-Semitism that National Socialism lives and breathes."

As 1934 began Barth's own position grew increasingly precarious. Helped on its way by Ludwig Müller a rumour spread that he was about to be dismissed from his teaching post in Bonn. This was almost true. The University authorities were considering his dismissal as he refused to open his lectures with the Hitler salute, now a requirement on University professors. When challenged by the authorities, he replied that he opened his lectures with a prayer, and that the requirement for the salute was a recommendation, not an order. In the unlikely event that he had left the authorities in any doubts as to his position, he wrote to both the Rector and the Minister of Cultural Affairs to let them know that even if the matter were to become an order he would not obey it.

The agitation against Barth grew ever stronger and more widespread. In Westphalia one congregation publicly, and at length, denounced his theology as a form of demonic magic which had taken possession of pastors and professors, whole congregations and worst of all many young theologians. There also now appeared a German Christian article which linked his theology with the popular belief that the German Army would have won the Great War had Germany not been stabbed in the back by civilian politicians, particularly Social Democrats. "During the War", the article declared "the church stood bravely with the field-grey Armies". Then, as a form of treason and defeatism there had emerged Barth's theology which "could not do enough to highlight the chasms that separate the Kingdom of

God from the State, and humanity from God." There is a great deal to be said for this German Christian definition of Barth's theology. In succinct form it sets out the attitude which many, indeed most, theologians have taken, and continue to take, to Barth's theology.

Barth did, however, manage to have a holiday early that year to France with Charlotte von Kirschbaum. In a Dominican monastery he had discussions with Catholic theologians and in Paris marvelled at the female dancers on the stage of the Casino de Paris. Watching the dancers, he wondered again at "the old question" of why it is that the church does not even try to be as good at what it does as "the children of this world".

In Paris, he gave a lecture in French, in which he described theology. "Of all disciplines, theology is the fairest, the one that moves the head and heart most fully, the one that comes closest to human reality, the one that gives the clearest perspective on the truth which every discipline seeks. It is a landscape like those of Umbria and Tuscany with views which are distant and yet clear, a work of art which is as well planned and as bizarre as the cathedrals of Cologne or Milan ... But of all disciplines, theology is also the most difficult and the most dangerous, the one in which a man is most likely to end in despair, or - and this is almost worse - in arrogance."

The objectives of the church opposition at the meeting with Hitler were Müller's resignation, the lifting of the decree which imposed the Aryan paragraph on the church and banned dissent, and the establishment of church-state relations which would protect the status of the Landeskirchen within a Reich Church. The church opposition had powerful allies. Not only Hindenberg, but almost half the Reich Cabinet were now sympathetic. Ludwig Müller however had an important ally in Hermann Göering. At that time Göering was, among other posts, Head of the Prussian Gestapo and he too had been busy preparing for the meeting with Hitler. This included having his Gestapo tap telephones.

A few days before the meeting with Hitler, representatives of the church opposition met to prepare a memorandum to Hitler as the written basis of their case. As well as the leaders of the League there were the three Bishops of the intact churches and theologians such as Gogarten. Barth had not been invited. A crucial point in the preparation of the memorandum was whether to break entirely with the German Christians or only with the excesses of the Movement, such as those displayed at the Sports Palace. Agreement was eventually reached that only the excesses be specifically condemned; the door should be left open to the moderate German Christians. A memorandum was then produced which began by thanking God for all he had done for the German People in the past year through Adolf Hitler. At this point there was an unwelcome interruption; Barth arrived. Someone, fearing compromise, had sent for him. On starting to read the memorandum he could not accept the opening reference to God, history and Hitler. This confirmed all his worst fears about the church opposition. Stung by his criticism a theologian, supported by Gogarten and most of the others, pointed out that the memorandum should thank God for the delivery of Germany from Bolshevism, for the massive fall in unemployment, and for the success of the Government's Winter Relief Programme.

For a moment the centuries rolled back as Barth hurled back words once used by Luther: "We have different beliefs, different spirits, and a different God". Above the din which followed Gogarten could be heard crying out that Barth could not be serious, and others that Barth be thrown out. Then wiser voices prevailed, inviting Barth to show Christian love and withdraw his insult. This plea succeeded in restoring quiet, thus enabling Barth to shout out that of course he was serious. Amid the uproar a Lutheran Bishop groaned that this was the end of the Protestant church in Germany.

The representatives of the Protestant church, including Ludwig Muller and the leaders of the church opposition, met with Adolf Hitler on 25th January 1934. Barth was not present. Before the meeting could even begin to discuss the items on the agenda, Göering opened his briefcase and took out his Gestapo files. First he read out the transcripts of a telephone conversation made by Niemöller that very morning and which could be interpreted as part of a political conspiracy to play Hindenberg off against Hitler. Then more material which alleged that the activities of the League were aimed against the State itself. Whether Hitler knew in advance of what Göering had to reveal is unknown. In any event Hitler immediately took control of, and dominated the proceedings. The protestations of patriotism and loyalty to the State from the representatives of the church opposition did not impress him. He would not put up with any political agitation. He pointed out that Ludwig Müller had not been chosen by him as Reich Bishop but by the church itself following its own free elections. The church must recognise that it alone bore full responsibility for its present problems. He appealed to all those present to attempt to behave in a "Christian and brotherly" way and try to collaborate together for the sake of the nation. If that failed and the church struggle continued, he would have no choice but to cut off all State support and funding for the church.

Then he shook everyone by the hand and left. Even years later during the Second World War, he could still call to mind, with malice and joy, the look on the faces of the church opposition.

Following the shock at the meeting with Hitler the church opposition fell apart in bitter internal recriminations, and the Bishops of the intact churches openly declared their loyalty and support for the Reich Bishop. Müller and his ally Jäger now pressed ahead with the final transformation of the German Evangelical Federation into a single Reich Church. The first of the Landeskirchen to be destroyed was the largest, the Old Prussian Union. By a decree of 1 March 1934, it was stripped of all independence and became the first building block of the Reich Church. More followed and by the time Hitler arrived at Tempelhof Airfield on 1st May 1934 to join in the celebrations of the achievement of the first year of his Thousand Year Reich, nearly three-quarters of all Protestants in Germany had been incorporated into the Reich Church. The remaining Landeskirchen were due to follow shortly.

All efforts by the church opposition having failed, here and there throughout the Pastors' Emergence League people now began to think in terms of a separate church, a Confessing Church. If, however, there were to be a proper Confessing Church there should first be a synod to consider a Confession as its basis. Some saw such a Synod and a possible Confession as an opportunity to make a final break with the German Christians. Others, particularly among the Lutherans, hoped such a Synod would re-unite the whole Church including all the German Christians.

Though born of mixed motives the movement to call a Synod grew and the "First Confessing Synod of the German Evangelical Church" was called for the end of May at Barmen with representatives from the League and the intact churches. The Synod would debate legal issues and if possible agree to a Confession of Faith. Due to certain Lutheran theological sensitivities the Confession would have to be called a Declaration. Three theologians would meet in advance of the Synod to prepare a draft Declaration for discussion. To reflect the national balance of numbers in the church, two would be Lutheran and one Reformed, the latter being Karl Barth.

There were 139 Delegates at the Synod of Barmen, drawn from all over Germany and with an average age of less than forty. As well as pastors, Bishops and church officials, the delegates included lawyers, engineers, manufacturers, physicians, businessmen, engineers, landowners, schoolteachers, a publisher, a farmer, a mine-inspector, a book-dealer, an architect and a cooper. George Mertz was there, as was Gertrude Staewen's brother-in-law Gustave Heinemann, later to become Chancellor of the German Federal Republic. There was only one woman among these delegates; that was not a time or place where women were encouraged to hold responsible positions. Confounding all easy judgements on the past and on people however, is the fact that Stephanie von Mackensen was not only a member of the Nazi Party but she went on to become a member of the governing body of the Confessing Church.

Barth was always fond of recalling how, fortified by strong coffee and Brazilian cigars, he wrote the whole of the Barmen Declaration while his two Lutheran colleagues slept away a three-hour lunch break. This is an exaggeration, and simplifies a rather more complex process. However the Lutherans did have a long lunch break and Barth was the author of the Barmen Declaration. His colleagues were at a disadvantage in any event; Barth had been planning for this for a long time. In retrospect one of the most surprising things about the Synod of Barmen is how anyone ever expected that Barth would have allowed anyone but himself to write the Declaration.

While the delegates knew that Barth was author of the Declaration it was not he who presented it to the open session of the Synod. This was providential. There were those present who heartily disliked both Barth and his theology. As for the Bishops, Marahrens regarded Barth as the main threat to the Protestant church in Germany, a view with which Bishop Meiser had growing sympathy. Besides, there were the ubiquitous speculations about Charlotte von Kirschbaum. To hear Barth speak in favour of his Declaration would, for some, have contained a degree of perhaps unacceptable provocation.

Unknown to the church opposition, the Synod of Barmen was only allowed to proceed on the basis of information supplied to the Gestapo by an informer. The Prussian Gestapo, now headed by Heinrich Himmler considered the church struggle such a serious threat to the unity of People and State that they viewed the calling of the Synod with considerable alarm. Then word came from an informer within the church opposition that, given the personalities involved and the fundamental differences between the various factions, the most likely outcome of the Synod would be the church opposition finally tearing itself to pieces. The Gestapo allowed the Synod to go ahead so as to provide that opportunity.

The Barmen Declaration was drafted in such a way that it would constitute a definition of the true church for those who agreed to it. There were six articles and they contained the essence of Barth's theology. Taken together they declared that the church cannot alter its witness so as to suit the state or any other power and that the church sets a limit to the power and claims of the state on its citizens. The articles were in the style of Reformation Confessions; scriptural texts, then a statement of what is confessed as true doctrine, followed by the condemnation of false doctrine. The foundations of the Declaration were set out in the first article.

"'I am the way, the truth and the life: no man commeth unto the Father but by me'. (John 14.6).

'Verily, verily, I say unto you, he that entereth not by the door into the sheep fold, but climbeth up some other way, the same is a thief and a robber... I am the door: by me if any man enter in, he shall be saved'. (John 10.1.9).

Jesus Christ, as he has testified to us in Holy Scripture is the one Word of God, who we are to hear, and who we have to trust and obey in life and in death.

We condemn the false doctrine that the Church can and must recognise as God's revelation other events and powers, forms and truths, apart from and alongside the one Word of God."

The Declaration was presented to the delegates in open session by Hans Asmussen, a pastor of Altona, who explained that it rejected historical events or, "culture, aesthetic sensibility, progress, or other powers and entities" as binding on the church. When we make Gods out of creatures, said Asmussen "they offer themselves to us as redeemers, but they prove to be the torturers of an unredeemed world". With the advantage of hindsight, these words carry the weight of prophesy.

The language of the Declaration can seem almost deliberately archaic, perhaps arcane even, a return to the language of the Reformation. Though perhaps in terms more familiar to Luther than ourselves there is a stark simplicity. No doubt is left that a demand is being made and a decision being called for. At Barmen, given all that had gone before in the church struggle, the delegates could have had little doubt as to what was being demanded of them and of the consequences, including personal consequences, of their individual decisions. After Asmussen had spoken, after the Declaration had been deliberated at length by the delegates, a vote was taken and the Declaration was unanimously approved. At this, some broke into tears of emotion, one jumped to his feet and started to sing a hymn and was followed by the others. More than forty years later, Sophie von Mackensen was to recall, "It was overwhelming, how we were given the words decided upon in Barmen. All at once we were freed from our isolation, and experienced a community that, until then, hadn't existed in the Evangelical church".

There had just taken place the most significant event in the Protestant church in Germany since the Reformation. The Synod had, in effect, proclaimed acceptance of the Barmen Declaration as the basis and mark of membership of the Confessing Church and that the Confessing Church was the true Protestant church. The Reich Church, the national Protestant church of the national socialist State was an impostor, a fake, and a false church, empty of substance and devoid of authority. To the end of his life, Karl Barth never ceased to be amazed at the outcome of the Synod of Barmen. That the Declaration had been unanimously agreed. Though he never used the term there is little doubt that he regarded it as nothing less than a miracle.

Later he regretted that the Declaration had a major omission; it did not include a specific condemnation of anti-semitism and persecution of the Jews. He doubted however whether even the delegates to the Synod of Barmen would have unanimously accepted such a condemnation.

Though in terms of numbers, the Confessing Church was to remain a minority at national level, there were parts of Germany where it became the majority. In Westphalia alone, half a million carried the red membership card of the Confessing Church. As the church grew, so did the attempts by the state to suppress it. In Mecklenberg, pastors were arrested and in a show trial sentenced to several months imprisonment. August Jäger seized control of two of the intact churches and arrested their Bishops. In face of the resulting outcry, he backed down and the Bishops were released. The following year, seven hundred pastors were placed under house arrest for denouncing from their pulpits the false Gods of race and People.

Though the German Evangelical Federation had been destroyed, the Reich Church was only a large but hollow shell. For Hitler, the outcome of the church struggle was a complete disaster; a defeat which, to a certain extent, he was pragmatic enough to accept. Attempts to suppress the Confessing Church and absorb it into the Reich Church eventually ceased; Ludwig Müller and the post of Reich Bishop were allowed to lapse into obscurity. State policy towards the Confessing Church and its members now became not one of absorption into the Reich Church but one of constant observation, petty restrictions and harassment. In some cases, more dramatic steps were taken. The sermons of Martin Niemöller grew ever louder in their denunciations of the injustices and tyranny of the state and in 1937 he was arrested on charges of inciting unrest and encouraging traitorist activities. The court found him guilty, but then only fined and released him. In fury, Hitler had Niemöller re-arrested as the personal prisoner of the Führer and sent to Sachenhausen concentration camp, then to Dachau, where he remained until 1945.

The Confessing Church was not a resistance movement to the national socialist state. Most of the members of the church remained the nationalistic and patriotic Germans they had always been. Some were members of the Nazi Party. The majority certainly did not wish the Confessing Church to become involved in any kind of political opposition to the state; they remained as loyal as any other Germans. Only a small minority came to see eventually that neither the discredited German Christians nor Ludwig Müller were the real enemy but that which stood behind them, the national socialist state itself. The only thing which united them all as members of the Confessing Church was their opposition, on the basis of the Barmen Declaration, to the demand that the ideology of the state also be decisive for their faith. At that time, in that state, in a Protestant church traditionally proud of its close ties to both throne and state this was remarkable, and at times brave, enough.

Both the achievements and limitations of the Confessing Church were to be set out by Charlote von Kirschbaum in a series of public addresses she gave in Switzerland towards the end of the Second World War. She began by pointing out that for a long time beforehand the Protestant church in Germany had proclaimed other messages and announced other kingdoms than that of God. "I am thinking for example of the kingdom of culture and of science, and also of that fateful of kingdom of German nationalism which reigned in the church long before Hitler. Then came the year 1933 when this cosy relationship between church and world was suddenly disrupted because the national socialist state reached out for the church, as it did for all areas of life, in order to force it into the service of the state. It wanted the church to "conform", just as the schools, the courts, the universities, and everything else had been made to conform." Contrary to this will to conform, the Confessing Church had been established and had "fought for the purity of its witness, its teaching ministry, its organisational structure, and its leadership." Despite this it must be admitted "that the Confessing Church, not out of a lack of courage but from a lack of insight, acted too timidly in defending and emphasising the ecclesiastical nature of its struggle. It was of the opinion that church and politics have nothing to do with each other and that the church would be denying its "proper task", which it had now begun to take seriously, if it involved itself directly in the issues of the state." This must be recognised as a limitation, a boundary of the church struggle. "But it must not be forgotten that the churches in Germany were in reality the only places where there was organised opposition to National Socialism. The brave resistance of innumerable individuals from other areas of society are also recognised. But if only all those other areas and institutions had defended their own concerns, things would have been very different in Germany today."

CHAPTER 16

After Barmen, tensions grew between Barth and those in the collective leadership of the Confessing Church who regarded the independence of the church as an end in itself. When the Third Confessing Synod was called, Bishop Meiser insisted that it take place only if Barth were neither invited nor present. He was not invited and he did not attend but on hearing a report on the debates of the Synod, he commented that the Confessing Church "still has no heart for the millions who suffer unjustly. It still has nothing to say on the simplest questions of public honesty. When it speaks it speaks only about its own affairs".

All public servants were now required to swear an oath of unconditional loyalty to the Führer. Barth was prepared to swear the oath provided it contained an addition to the effect that he could be loyal to the Führer only within his responsibilities as a Christian. He was therefore dismissed from his Bonn post in November 1934. Pressure had been mounting against him for a while. Earlier in the year he had been cross-examined by the Gestapo about remarks made to the Pastors' Emergence League the previous autumn in Berlin and for a period had been placed under "city arrest", unable to leave Bonn.

Though his case appeared hopeless, he challenged his dismissal in the courts. A request to the leadership of the Confessing Church for their formal support in his appeal was refused. Only now did he appreciate the extent and depth of the opposition to him even in the Confessing Church itself. In March 1935, while his appeal was proceeding through the Courts he was approached by the Gestapo in the railway station at Bonn and told there was now a total ban on his speaking in public. In June the courts reached their decision on his appeal. He was fined a fifth of his salary for refusing the give the Hitler salute and for making anti-State remarks but the Courts squashed his dismissal from the Bonn post. At this, the Minister for Cultural Affairs directly intervened and, using special powers available to him, banned Barth from holding any public post in Germany. Together with Nelly Barth, their children and Charlotte von Kirschbaum, he left for Switzerland. Bishop Marahrens, the Lutheran Bishop of Hanover, was no doubt not the only person glad to see the back of Barth but it was he who had the distinction, in the pastoral letter sent to the members of his church, of providing material for the gossips. "We may wonder whether Karl Barth was not influenced much more than he realised by the peculiar circumstances of his private life, rather than being basically influenced by the Holy Scriptures. Not a few persons would regard this as a painful tragedy".

In Switzerland Barth took up a post at Basle University and from the windows of his house on the Albanring he could see, as a daily reminder of Germany, the last outrunners of the Black Forest. He never ceased to warn the Churches in Europe of the dangers of Hitler and National Socialism. In Germany all his writings were put on the Index of Prohibited Books. When in 1938 Hitler threatened Czechoslovakia he wrote to the leaders of the Reformed Church there urging them to support armed resistance to any German attack. This provoked outrage in the German press with such headlines as "Professor of Theology is Warmonger" and "Jews – Czechs – Karl Barth". The leaders of the Confessing Church published a formal letter of censure against him.

In the early summer of 1940 Karl Barth's brother Peter died. That morning there had come news of the French army falling back before the German advance. In his final moments Peter had cried out "But we will not withdraw beyond the Loire". A few months later Karl Barth wrote in a letter to church leaders in now Occupied France: "Yet you, and we with you, had to withdraw far, far beyond the Loire." In a later letter to church leaders in Britain he explained that he wrote on a day in which victorious Nazi troops "are marching against Mount Olympus and at the same time against the Pyramids and who knows whether they may not one day march against Mount Sinai." During the late nineteen thirties he had been dismayed that having for so long spoken the language of nationalism and militarism the churches throughout western Europe, as Nazism grew stronger, were busily discovering the virtues of neutrality and pacifism. He did not doubt that "the well-known arguments for Christian pacifism, which twenty-five years ago we made our own or which at any rate deeply disturbed us, may later, in a different situation and in a different form, bring us under their power." But for now, they had no such power. He asked the churches throughout Europe to recognise that National Socialism was not just another political experiment but a movement which demanded unconditional love and obedience. Saint Paul had seen in the state a fallible human institution, but one which could set human boundaries to much of the hurt we do to each other and had, in his first Letter to Timothy, exhorted Christians to pray for the state so that we all "may lead a quiet and peaceable life in all Godliness and honesty". The National Socialist state, being both anarchy and a tyranny, is the enemy of those all too human and fallible arrangements which we are asked to pray for. Now that this state was attacking its neighbour this was no time for the churches to be seeking refuge and deliverance in the neutrality of pacifism.

In letters and speeches urging resistance he also tried to explain that Christians would be wrong to imagine that in doing so they are fighting some kind of holy war. They are "not creating or hastening the Kingdom of God; that is entirely God's own affair. If Christians realise this they will be spared those perceptions and disappointments which result from vain expectations. The churches certainly ought not to persuade the democratic States that they are, so to say, the Lord's own warriors. But they ought to say to them that we are privileged to be *human* and that we must *defend* ourselves with the power of desperation against the inbreaking of open inhumanity."

Working on behalf of refugees he was appalled when the Swiss authorities amended the law to make it more difficult for Jewish refugees to find sanctuary in Switzerland. "The Rhine will not wash away our guilt for having turned away ten thousand fugitives and having treated unworthily those who we did accept".

In speeches in 1941 to large audiences he warned that Switzerland was facing the danger that" the great steamroller of the so-called re-ordering of Europe will eventually on one of its tours also certainly reach this corner which, up till now, has still been spared." His audience was invited to picture Switzerland under Nazi rule where the new rulers "would make it a daily moral principle to destroy" all those who offered resistance. The meaning and substance, the innermost centre of the Nazi Empire consisted "in the hatred and repudiation of the Jew ... But the Son of Man, who was the Son of God, was a Jew."

The danger he feared most likely was not military invasion but Switzerland all too easily accommodating itself to the demands of Nazi Germany particularly as regards war materials and economic and political support. He described the danger and temptation facing his country. "Switzerland could ... lose its character as a community of free states unified by justice; it could cease ... to be the memory of the old and the hope of the new order of Europe. It could become a corner of the world about which nothing more than this would be said: that there are all kinds of large and small people here who, more or less, earn their money, and who happen to have fun. ... The inhabitants of our cantons are no longer free, they have become herds who, though they are diligently working and happily enjoying themselves, are at the same time, irresponsible."

If this came to pass it would not make any difference whether Hitler invaded or not. Switzerland would have become a cog in Hitler's war machine. Barth's audience of several thousand was then asked whether or not this was already happening. Not only in the continuing supply of war materials to Germany but with the advance to the Nazi Government of nearly 1 billion Swiss francs. Was not the Swiss Government already making itself the financial backer of Nazi Germany "and in this respect also an accomplice in the war".

Such speeches enraged the German government who made formal protests to Switzerland. Even the Swiss Ambassador in Berlin demanded that the Berne Authorities "put a muzzle on Barth". The member of Zofingia who nearly 40 years before had opposed Barth on the social question was now Federal Minister of Justice and ordered an illegal tap on Barth's telephone. Consideration was given to arresting and imprisoning Barth but the outcome was that in the summer of 1941 he was banned from making political speeches anywhere in Switzerland.

Among other wartime activities was the sending of money to Gertrude Staewen in Berlin. At first for her to pass on to those in the Confessing Church who would use it to help Jews, then for the activities of a resistance group formed by her and some of her friends. The group arranged forged documents for Jews trying to leave Germany and even tried to bribe a Gestapo official to arrange the release of some Jews already in the camps. Though the group was eventually uncovered, Gertrude Staewen received a warning that the police were on their way to arrest her and was able to escape Berlin to assume a new life in Leipzig then in Weimar. At the end of the war she made her way to the nearby Buchenwald concentration camp to try to discover whether any of her friends had survived the Third Reich.

Charlotte von Kirschbaum was Barth's companion in all his political activities and as a German national living in Switzerland she put herself in a position of considerable risk. One crisis came in 1943 when the German Embassy made an attempt, ultimately unsuccessful, to have her sent back to Germany. Undeterred by such proximity to danger she joined in 1944 the leadership of the Committee for a Free Germany.

Established to "struggle against the Fascist war effort and to seek for ways to establish a free independent Germany", its activities violated the police relations governing foreigners in Switzerland and the meetings had to be held in secret. Such clandestine political activity was even more dangerous by reason of the fact that most of the others in the leadership were members of the Communist Party. On one occasion Barth arranged a meeting at his home between them and some Protestant émigrés. He had to admit this had not been a success. "Unfortunately the Christian émigrés did not show up well in contrast to the much greater simplicity and the goodwill of the others, who claimed to be atheists but in reality reacted in a much more Christian manner."

In January and February 1945, as the Allied armies advanced into Germany itself, Barth spoke in a number of Swiss towns about the need for a new beginning in Germany. This speech was, in effect, his last word in the church struggle and reminded his Swiss audience of what Christ was at that moment saying to the Germans.

"Come to me, you heartless ones, you wicked Hitler Youth, you brutal SS soldiers, you vicious Gestapo villains, you sorry compromisers and collaborators, you mass men who for so long patiently and stupidly followed your so-called leader. Come to me, you guilty ones, you who share the guilt and who are now learning, and have to learn, what your deeds are worth. Come to me, I know you well, but I do not ask who you are or what you have done. I see only that you are at an end and for good or ill must begin again; I will refresh you, I will now begin again from the very beginning with you. If the Swiss, puffed up with their democratic, social, and Christian ideas, which they have always extolled, are not interested in you, I am. If they will not say it, I will say it: I am for you, I *am* your friend".

As for Emmanuel Hirsch he had played a vigorous and aggressive role in attempting to prevent Confessing Church members from gaining any standing in the theological faculties of the universities. With the fall of the Third Reich in 1945, he was forcibly retired from his own university post and refused a pension. He also began to lose his sight. Though poor and nearly blind, he did not give way to despair. In an effort to support himself, he tried to write a novel. It sold, he wrote another and so Emmanuel Hirsch became the successful author of historical novels. One concerned Huguenot refugees fleeing to safety in

Germany from religious persecution in France.   Financially secure, he was able once more to deploy that incredible erudition which had so amazed Barth when they first met at Göttingen and he produced several works of theological and historical scholarship which are among the most outstanding of the 20th century. His unquestioned brilliance, and the fact that he outlived all his contemporaries, led eventually to Hirsch being called "The Last Prince" of Protestant theology.   Though he never spoke about politics, it was unlikely he ever changed his fundamental views. Neither his brilliance nor his erudition, nor his undoubted courage in physical adversity, could however prevent a degree of private ridicule. Until his death, it was whispered behind his back that he kept a portrait of Adolf Hitler in his basement.

In 1946, Barth was invited back to Bonn to give a series of lectures. As he travelled down the Rhine in the splendour of spring on a Swiss freighter, the river unwound a procession of sunken ships, broken bridges and shattered cities. At Bonn, walking up from the river into the city, he was met by Günter Dehn who laughed and chatted and seemed the same as ever. As Barth delivered his lectures at the university, there came through the windows the rattling of machinery as the semi-ruined buildings were torn down in preparation for rebuilding. While poking about among the rubble one day, he discovered an undamaged bust of Schleiermacher and had it restored to a place of honour.

BIBLIOGRAPHY

ALLAN, CHARLES – The Beautiful Thing That Has Happened
To Our Boys.
(Greenock: McKelvie 1915)

BARNETT, VICTORIA - For The Soul Of The People. Protestant
Protest Against Hitler
(Oxford University Press. New York. 1992.)

BARTH, KARL – Theological Existence Today
(Hodder and Stoughton. London. 1933.)

BARTH, KARL – Protestant Theology in The Nineteenth
Century.
(SCM Press. London. 1972.)

BARTH, KARL – The Word of God and the Word of Man
(Hodder and Stoughton. London. 1928.)

BARTH, KARL – The Epistle to the Romans
(Oxford University Press. London. 1933.)

BARTH, KARL – The German Church Conflict
(Lutterworth. London. 1965.)

BARTH, KARL – A Letter to Great Britain from Switzerland.
(London. 1941 The Sheldon Press.)

BARTH, KARL – A Karl Barth Reader
(T&T Clark Ltd. Edinburgh. 1986.)

BARTH, KARL – Church Dogmatics. Vol 1 : Part One
(T&T Clark Ltd. Edinburgh 1975.)

BERGEN, DORIS L. – Twisted Cross.
(The University of North Carolina Press. 1996.)

BUSCH, EBERHARD – Karl Barth
(SCM Press. London. 1976.)

COCHRANE, ARTHUR C. – The Church's Confession Under Hitler.
(The Westminster Press. Philadelphia 1962)

ERICKSEN, ROBERT P. – Theologians Under Hitler.
(Yale University Press. New Haven & London. 1985.)

HOYLE, R. BIRCH – The Teaching of Karl Barth.
(SCM Press. London 1930.)

JEHLE, FRANK – Ever Against The Stream.
(William B. Erdmaus. Grand Rapids/Cambridge 2002.)

JOHNSON, PAUL – A History of Christianity.
(Weiderfeld & Nicholson. London 1976)

JUNGER, ERNST – Storm of Steel
(Chatto and Windus. London 1929)

KŐBLER, RENATE – In the Shadow Of Karl Barth.
(Westminster/John Knox Press. Louisville. 1989.)

LACARRIERE, JACQUES – The Gnostics
(Peter Owens. London 1977)

LAWRENCE, D. H. – Phoenix
(Heinemann. London. 1936.)

McCORMACK, BRUCE L. – Karl Barths' Critically Realistic Dialectical Theology.
(Clarendon Press. Oxford. 1995.)

MACKINTOSH, H. R. – Types of Modern Theology : Schliermacher to Barth.
(Nisbet. London. 1937.)

MATHESON, PETER – The Third Reich and the Christian Churches.
(T&T Clark. Edinburgh. 1981.)

SCHOLDER, KLAUS – The Churches and The Third Reich.
(SCM Press 1987 and 1988)

SHINER, LARRY – The Secularisation of History
(Nashville/New York. 1966.)

SIMMONS, MICHAEL – Berlin. The Dispossessed City.
(Hamish Hamilton. London 1988)

SMART, JAMES D. – Revolutionary Theology in the Making.
Barth – Thurneysen Correspondence 1914 – 1925.
(John Knox Press. Richmond Virginia. 1964.)

SPENDER, STEPHEN - World Within World.
(Hamish Hamilton. London. 1951.)

THOMSON, JOHN (Editor) – Theology Beyond Christendom.
(Pickwick Publications. Allison Park, Pennsylvania. 1986.)

TUCHMAN, BARBARA – The Guns of August.
(Constable and Co. London. 1962.)